T0146629

THE MEANING OF
SHINTO

BY
J.W.T. MASON

FOREWORD TO REPRINT BY
REV. ANN LLEWELLYN EVANS

 www.trafford.com

North America & international
toll-free: 1 888 232 4444 (USA & Canada)
fax: 812 355 4082

FOREWORD

TO THE REPRINT OF

THE MEANING OF SHINTO

A highly regarded scholar of Shinto, J.W.T. Mason published *The Meaning of Shinto* in 1935 presenting his views of spirituality, mythology, and creativity as they relate to Shinto. Mason (1879 to 1941) was an American journalist who published several works on eastern spiritual traditions, including *The Creative East* and *Creative Freedom*.

In searching for books on Shinto from a spiritual rather than academic perspective, I found Mason's work presents rare insight not only into the basic beliefs of Shinto, but also into the importance of mythology and creativity to the evolution of our understanding of life and the universe. Unfortunately, Mason's works are now out-of-print and therefore difficult to find. Thus, I have chosen to reprint *The Meaning of Shinto* to make this important and perceptive work available to readers.

This edition of *The Meaning of Shinto* is a re-publication of Mason's original text; the unedited content has been maintained in its original style, spelling, and punctuation.

Mason begins by establishing his view of the development of man, language, and spiritual expression. According to Mason, early man had an innate, intuitive understanding of the universe and the order that existed even prior to his own existence. This perception existed prior to man's ability to express himself through language.

As language developed, these concepts were expressed through stories and ritual, reflecting a conscious expression of subconscious knowledge. Early man's subconscious understanding of truth thus surfaced through mythology, ritual, art, music, and dance. Detailed analysis and dissection of these expressions would be a process similar to intellectual description and analysis of an artist's work: the underlying feel and truth would be lost. Instead, modern man will better receive the meaning of the myth, ritual, or artwork if we look beyond the literal words and presentation, allowing ourselves to experience the message intuitively.

Mason maintains that Shinto tradition has made relatively few altera-
tions to the original mythology and ritual practices from thousands of
years ago. As a result, the experience of Shinto is closer to early man's
intuitive roots than many other traditions.

Shinto recognizes a certain order to the universe wherein all of life
stems from the same original source. Therefore, Shinto considers all
creation to be of divine origin; this sweeping concept includes spiritual
beings, mankind, other living beings, plants, mountains, oceans, etc. Man
thus is part of a much larger picture, referred to in Japanese as *Dai Shizen*
or Great Nature.

The central theme throughout Shinto is to recognize this natural harmony and to reestablish an accord through return to the natural way, a
return to the path of Great Nature.

Shinto does not, however, have a doctrine or sacred directive which
tells us specifically how to accomplish this. Instead, it challenges us to
find the correct path through prayer, ritual, and practice. Shinto ritual
exists to enable this connection, to allow one to explore his/her unconscious and intuitive understanding of existence as well as, in Jungian
terms, to experience the "collective unconscious" of mankind.

This requires great sincerity, focus, and creativity on the part of each
person. In western terms, we might also refer to this as "free will," since
Shinto does not recognize any omnipotent deity who directs the fate of
mankind. In Chapter III of this text, Mason explains the origins of the
kanji for the term "Shinto." While it is widely known that the term
"Shinto" means "the way or path of the kami," Mason goes even further
in explaining the evolution of the kanji pictograph itself, showing that,
"Shinto can mean: Kami man (or man as Kami) at the divine cross-road
choosing his way. The 'divine' cross-road means all the universe is divine spirit."

This foundation of free will, or "man choosing his way," means that
life is a creative process. Our path is not pre-destined; it evolves. Thus,
our participation in any spiritual tradition, as well as in Shinto specifically,
calls for a dynamic response. Although we may rely on and practice
ancient rituals and traditions, as mankind develops intellectually, we must
deepen our conscious understanding. We are not to take mythological
and spiritual rites and cast them into stone, thus degrading their
expression. Nor should we try and change these practices as a result of
intellectual or conscious analysis. Instead, we must reach beyond our
intuition and allow for a certain mindfulness to deepen our spiritual
experience.

This is, I believe, what Shinto offers to us. As the reader will see through Mason's writings, Shinto has deep-seated traditions and rituals which allow both connection to ancient intuition and, because of its lack of specified doctrine, also allows modern creative response. The written word can become formalized and inflexible to the changing needs of society. In Shinto, great responsibility is instead placed on the individual to search his/her heart for truth and correctness through prayer and ritual, a process requiring dynamic, creative response.

One particular individual, Guji Yukitaka Yamamoto, has taken a giant step in this direction by introducing Shinto to the western world. Guji Yamamoto is High Priest of Tsubaki Grand Shrine of Mie Prefecture, Japan, a shrine over 2000 years old. Guji Yamamoto introduced Shinto to the western world by establishing a branch shrine in America in 1987. Tsubaki Grand Shrine of America, now located in Granite Falls, Washington has visitors from across North America and from a multitude of ethnic backgrounds. Another branch recently opened in British Columbia, Canada—Bright Woods Spiritual Centre—also receives visitors from a variety of backgrounds seeking to learn Shinto practice.

Shinto is an ancient tradition that is vital for modern people. I hope that each reader will find in Mason's *Meaning of Shinto* not only an insightful explanation of Shinto beliefs and ritual, but also a challenge to individuals of any spiritual tradition that their religious experience remain rooted in ancient, intuitive wisdom while simultaneously developing conscious understanding and contemporary expression.

—Ann Llewellyn Evans
Shinto Priestess
Director, Matsuri Foundation

THE MEANING OF
SHINTO

THE PRIMAEVAL FOUNDATION OF
CRATIVE SPIRIT IN MODERN JAPAN

BY
J.W.T. MASON
Author of "The Creative East," "Creative Freedom," etc.

TO
THE MEMORY OF
SUJIN SUMERA MIKOTO

CONTENTS

PREFACE

THE author wishes to thank friends in all parts of Japan who have shown him unfailing kindness and have always been so patient in helping him to understand something of the inner character of the Japanese spirit. Not so much by verbal explanations but by attitudes, conduct and the normal activities of life and responses to environment have the Japanese people shown the author their understanding of the meaning of Shinto. The author has tried to translate into words what this meaning is, in some of its fundamental aspects. Where he has failed, the fault is his. If he has been able to reflect the spirit of Shinto in some small way it is because the Japanese people themselves have shown him where the rays fall by their own reactions.

Shinto is simple in its outward forms but has profound inward significance. The Japanese have never tried to make Shinto self-expressive in objective analytical ways but have been content to let the inner spirit of Shinto guide them as an integral part of themselves. If a being from another planet, having a different digestive system from our own, were to visit this earth and were to ask anyone how food taken into the mouth becomes converted into energy that keeps the body alive, nobody could answer him. Yet, the fact is there. So, when Western people, having a different conception of spirituality, ask Japanese what Shinto means, it does not imply Shinto has no meaning when Japanese reply that they do not know what the meaning is. The reply shows only that the Japanese have not analysed Shinto. Its power as a creative impetus, a stimulus of spiritual and mental energy for the people of Japan, has endured in the past, regardless of the lack of verbal explanations.

In 1874, a discussion of Shinto took place at a meeting of the Asiatic Society of Japan *(Proceedings,* Vol. II) at which Sir Harry Parkes, the British Minister, "expressed the disappointment which he in common with others had felt in being unable to learn what Shintoism was. Japanese in general seemed utterly at a loss to describe it, but this circumstance was intelligible if what was once an indigenous faith had been turned in later days into a political engine. . . . Rev. Dr. Brown said ... it would be strange if during a residence of more than fourteen years in Japan he had not endeavoured to inform himself upon this subject but as had been said by the President, Dr. Hepburn, his search for information in the literature of the country had been poorly rewarded, unless he counted the discovery of the emptiness of Shintoism as a compensation for his pains. The Japanese books in which he had hoped to find something that would command his respect had utterly disappointed him. . . . The Government tacitly confesses that Shintoism is a vapid, lifeless thing when it sends men to preach throughout the country and provides them with texts taken from no Japanese sacred book but borrowed from Confucius and Mencius."

This point of view has prevailed generally among Westerners in Japan to the present time. Yet, Shinto works. One of the first actions of the Japanese, accompanying territorial expansion, is to erect Shinto Shrines. Nobody who has moved among the Japanese people and who has seen their attitude of respect, from the highest to the lowest, at Shinto Shrines can doubt the profound inner power of Shinto. This fact is baffling to Western mentalities that believe nothing exists until it is explained; but that is no reason for considering Shinto to be vapid and lifeless. The great moral and spiritual doctrines of the West and the East have all been analysed, but Shinto avoids doctrines and has remained isolated. It is the one national foundation of a great culture that has not been explained in modern terms. We know far more about the significance of the conceptions of ancient Egypt, dead for thousands of years, than about the significance of Shinto which is the most virile factor in the life of Japan.

If the present volume contributes in some small way to an understanding of the meaning of Shinto and stimulates others to investigate its inner implications, the author will be well rewarded. Shinto is neither a political expedient nor a prop for any special form of administration. Attempts to use it such-wise cannot confine Shinto, which is universal in its spiritual concepts. The Japanese people have brought Shinto from the dark of primaevalism into the light of modern progress. It is the nation's possession. It is the one enduring National Treasure. But, Shinto must not be buried in a museum of the mind. The Japanese people must begin to understand Shinto self-consciously. The more they do so the more will the West understand Japan. The West is lamentably ignorant of Japan; but, Japan, too, is ignorant, self-consciously, of herself. There was no Chair of Japanese History at Tokyo Imperial University until the decade of the Spanish-American War, and no Chair of Shinto until after the World War.

The Japanese say it is impossible to understand Japan without understanding Shinto. This is true for the West. How much more true is it of the Japanese people themselves! Shinto is understood intuitively by Japan; but until Japan understands Shinto self-consciously, the nation cannot explain itself to the West. Every nation must know how to explain itself to other nations in the new world that is dawning. Those that cannot do so will be left behind. Japan has been lamentably lacking in competence to explain herself. For the future welfare of this great nation of the Orient, where alone in the East the spirit of creative action exists in modern measure, the people must learn to understand their own culture more objectively. Shinto can be made Japan's major contribution to world culture, but Japan does not yet know how to offer the contribution. Shinto has a message for the world. It is for Japan to undertake the mission of spreading the message by making Shinto more realistic among the Japanese themselves. Awake, Japan, to this responsibility, which rests on all the people! Shinto belongs to the people. The problem of its increasing influence is theirs to solve.

J. W. T. M.

Tokyo

CHAPTER I

JAPAN'S CREATIVE SPIRIT

THE power of enduring progress in Japan is derived from the creative spirit of the race which expresses its individualistic and co-ordinating impetus in Shinto, a primaeval subconscious intuition that conceives humanity and Nature as divine spirit self-creating material progress without omnipotent guidance. To know Japan it is necessary to understand Shinto. But, to know Shinto is difficult because Shinto is not a self-consciously evolved creed. As the creative impetus is buried in the subconscious knowledge life has of itself, so is Shinto. Shinto is, indeed, the creative impetus interpreting itself in spiritual terms, not analytically, but by implications and direct responses to life. The Japanese have held fast to Shinto as the inner core of their culture from mythological times to the present; so to interpret Shinto by its results, the general tendencies of Japan's cultural development must be understood.

Shinto has given to Japan the consciousness of self-reliance and confidence in action, and has stimulated the Japanese mentality to interest itself in every aspect of life, for all existence, to Shinto, is divine spirit. At the same time, the fact that Shinto is so predominantly subconscious has resulted in Japanese culture progressing not as much by self-conscious examination as by intuitive feelings and an eagerness to try new ways whatever their origin. So, Japanese often have moved forward, somewhat impetuously, without waiting for adequate preparation. At times they have dissipated energy trying to inflict foreign ideas on themselves before properly understanding them, necessitating their later abandonment. Japanese have stumbled and fallen many times in pursuit of progress; but they usually fall forward and not backward, and they never lie prostrate nor bemoan their injuries. They always rise to put forth fresh effort, for Shinto showed them in the distant beginnings of their history that man must rely on experience and experiment for self-development and not wait for futile aid from supernatural sources.

The genius of Henri Bergson has given to the world an understanding of the creative impetus which provides the key to interpreting the character of Japan's creative evolution and the power of Shinto. The creative impetus is the spontaneous impulse of life seeking freedom of action. It is not a magical formula nor an omnipotent machine. It does not know new ways of progress in advance but must test them by results. The creative impetus ever seeks to expand by its own efforts; but life may grow tired of the difficulties and pains of effort and so may halt the quest for progress, resting content in mechanistic ways and in inherited habits. Such a desertion of the cause of creative action leads to cultural death. A culture lives by generating the new and uniting the new with old ways of proven worth, whereby continuity of national expansion is preserved. The creative impetus produces something out of nothing adding to past inheritances values that never before existed:

> It is true that nothing ever arises out of absolutely nothing. There is always something out of which it grows. But that does not explain it wholly. It does not account for the *new* in it. It is only in so far as it is still the old, or the old over again, that it is accounted for by what it grows out of. In so far as it is new, it remains unaccountable, unpredictable, uncontrolled, undetermined, free. *That* factor in it, therefore, *has* arisen out of nothing, and Novelty as such *means* Creation out of nothing. ... A world that generates novelty *is* creating itself out of nothing. It must be pronounced capable of arising out of nothing; only we must add that the creative process is still continuing.[1]

On this principle, the Shinto conception of creativeness, the primaeval spiritual intuition of Japan, must take its stand to be adequately understood. The creation of something out of nothing in Shinto does not mean everything was created out of nothingness at the beginning of existence. It means "the creative process is still continuing." Such is the way Japanese development has come into being and continues to change with changing conditions of life. Never has the creative impetus been absent from Japan's national life, though it has had to struggle at times against adverse mechanistic tendencies. Novelty, the absolutely new, has always had an irresistible fascination for the Japanese people, and never have they feared to try to make something new grow out of the old.

Japanese still are living who were born and had their early education in the nation's mediaeval era. Modern history has been making itself slowly in the West from the time of Columbus more than four hundred years of adjustment to scientific progress. The same co-ordinations have

---

[1]   F. C. S. Schiller, "Novelty," Presidential Address before the Aristotelian Society (London), October 10, 1921.

been made in Japan in less than a single lifetime. When a nation can change so quickly and successfully from mediaevalism to the modern scientific age, only one explanation is possible: the people have always been under the disciplined influence of the creative impetus. It is impossible suddenly to invoke creative power, in a crisis, unless it is already present within a culture. The creative impetus is not a force outside life; its presence within a nation is shown by the nation's competence to adapt itself to conditions of existence new to past conceptions, and to generate something out of nothing. This is what Japan was able to do when the nation was opened to the West in the middle of the Nineteenth Century; but the ability to make the changes had been developed long centuries before, due to the Shinto intuition of flexibility not binding man to any surface creed and keeping the subconscious mind free from prejudices.

Japan was long compelled to take the initiative in stimulating the creative impetus by herself alone, for there have been no competitions among rival civilizations in the Orient to aid her. In the West, the creative impetus has gained much of its strength from the challenges and interchanges among contending nations, in close relationships with one another. Under this condition of rivalry, more survival values are thrown to the surface and undergo harder tests and are subjected to wider analysis than when countries are not interested in learning from one another or are not forced into flexibility by threats against their existence. The West has increased its common store of knowledge from the time of Ancient Greece to the present by being able to draw upon its divergent ways of progress, carrying the results across frontiers for examination and practical trials and readjustments under many different conditions of life.

The Orient has not had this same advantage. The nations of the East have been far more self-contained than Occidental countries. It is possible to speak of a continuity of Western civilization for more than twenty-five hundred years; but in no such sense has there been a continuity of Oriental civilization. The major Oriental countries have gone their own ways with little interchange of values. Japan alone, in the Orient, has consistently followed the creative life movement of the West, continuously learning from others while at the same time preserving her own unique national identity. Long before Japan was known to the West, the people acquired broadened cultural influences that originated in India and China. But the other Oriental nations did not add to their creative powers from one another. India influenced China for a time through Buddhism, but debasement, not creative growth, followed. India took nothing of importance from China, and neither India nor China considered Japanese culture worthy of study.

Japan could have taught the rest of the Orient the secret of flexible progress and disciplined creative action; but the other countries of the East became hardened in their individualistic sophistications. If the rest of the Orient had shown an interest in the Japanese spirit of creative activity at all commensurate with Japan's interest in distant civilizations, the Orient today would be reverberating with vital energy. It is true that there has always been more self-expression on the Asiatic continent than in Japan, making it less difficult to understand the fundamentals of Chinese and Indian cultures than to discover the secluded springs of Japan's creative impetus; but this does not explain the continent's neglect of the insular interpretations of life. The static conditions of the continental cultures were due to their self-sufficiency. China occupied herself predominantly with an unprecedented expansion of aestheticism, while India devoted the more vital part of her energy to spiritual speculations. Each country has made invaluable contributions to the world by its exclusive genius, but both have suffered gravely themselves because of the lack of balance in their cultures.

Japan's initiative in seeking new sources of cultural inspiration was due to the nation's interest in versatility of self-development, acquired from the Shinto vision of the entire universe as being interrelated through the spiritual origin of all of its parts. Japan co-ordinated spirituality and aestheticism with utilitarianism, and progressed by holding the creative impetus faithful to these three spheres of versatility. This is one of Japan's gifts to world civilization: the example of a nation that has sustained itself under the rigid scientific requirements of modern material progress while at the same time amalgamating aesthetic and primaeval spiritual understandings of life with utilitarian efficiency. When a culture remains loyal to this ideal of development it cannot decay nor be destroyed by internal forces. The test of permanent creative progress for every country is its competence to increase its efficiency in material ways of progress while developing also its aesthetic and spiritual sensitiveness. For perhaps two thousand years Japan had striven to keep the three specializations of life united in her culture. Such a result cannot be achieved unless the creative impetus is always present, concerning itself with its own versatile effectiveness. At the same time, without the subconscious impetus of Shinto giving spiritual values to the blossoming of all Nature as well as to man's personality and to his material activities, no such co-ordinating impulse would have been possible for the Japanese people.

The Shinto influence, however, has been individualistic as well as co-ordinating. Individual desire for action, individual sense of responsibility, individual self-development have always been Japanese characteristics. Yet, the intuition of co-ordination has never been lost. The struggle between individualism and co-ordination dominates the entire course of Japanese history, revealing the creative impetus continuously seeking to adjust these two essential factors of human relationships to each other under changing conditions of progress. For every nation this is the primary proof of vital power and flexibility. How to retain individual freedom of action and yet not permit disintegration of national life; how to adjust the individual to the whole for the wider good of all and for higher attainments by the whole is the most baffling problem of progress:

> Society, which is the community of individual energies, benefits from the efforts of all of its members and renders effort easier to all. It can only subsist by subordinating the individual, it can only progress by leaving the individual free: contradictory requirements, which have to be reconciled. . . . Struggling among themselves and at war with one another, they (human societies) are seeking clearly, by friction and shock, to wear out antagonisms, to eliminate contradictions, to bring about that individual wills should insert themselves in the social will without leaving their individual form, and that different and diverse societies should enter in their turn into a wider and more inclusive society and yet not lose their originality or their independence. The spectacle is both disquieting and reassuring, for we cannot contemplate it without saying that here, too, across innumerable obstacles, life is working both by individualization and integration to obtain the greatest quantity, the richest variety, the highest qualities of invention and effort.[2]

Life, struggling in this way for its own advancement, by friction and shock among human societies, follows the same method within single nationalities as well. When any culture makes little effort to develop both individualism and integration, the creative impetus is dormant in the nation. When the creative impetus strives to expand in any nation, struggle between individualism and co-ordination ensues, for it is only by means of experiment and experience that life knows how to make adequate adjustments. Japan alone, in the Orient, has undergone this process of creative evolution as a continuing movement, increasing in complexity with the progressive advance of civilization.

---

[2] Henri Bergson, Mind-Energy, translated by H. Wildon Carr, pp. 33-4.

Family groupings, in the early history of Japan, threatened to suppress individual energies by making the common people, not free citizens, but "practically the property"[3] of the *Uji* or the family-clan, which exercised absolute control over its members. Group co-ordination lodged great power in the hands of the clan chiefs, placing nationalism in rivalry with the clans; and the Soga family became the dominant factors in this swing toward disintegration. The Japanese creative impetus, however, moved to check the denationalizing tendency. Shotoku Taishi, the great Regent of the Sixth-Seventh Centuries, promulgated a charter of human rights in his Seventeen Article Constitution, at a time when Europe was in the Dark Ages. Part of his purpose was to release the people from the autocratic sway of the *Uji,* and give individualism more freedom by transferring the *Uji* authority to the Throne. This expansive development attained its objective in the Daika Reforms, a quarter of a century later, giving civic solidity to Japan eight centuries before the rise of nationalism in the West at the time of Joan of Arc.

The Soga leaders of the family-clan movement went down before the liberalizing onslaught. For a time, individualistic growth flourished, but co-ordination gradually gained the upper hand. The powerful Fujiwara family, which had played a decisive role in overwhelming the Soga domination, eventually became supreme in controlling public affairs. The Fujiwara used their influence through marriage into the Imperial Family, to govern as they pleased. They encircled the Throne, threatening to subordinate the Emperor to their monopolistic ambitions. Had such a compression of the new nationalism endured, it would have imposed a mechanistic regime of irresponsible absolutism on Japan, throttling the spirit of creative action. But, the creative impetus of the race was too vigorous to submit to such a fate, and the Fujiwara despotism was overthrown, in turn, through the regeneration of individualistic effort in the provinces, due especially to rivalries between the Taira and Minamoto clans.

The field for individualism was further widened when the Minamoto forces crushed the Taira, and Minamoto Yoritomo, one of the most creative statesmen in world history, established the Shogunate system of government at the end of the Twelfth Century. Yoritomo is the only administrator the world has known who devised a political system which was not the outcome of an evolutionary process but was spontaneously original. It was so well suited to its environment that it endured until

---

[3] F. Brinkley, History of the Japanese People, p. 142.

Japan entered modern constitutional life in the middle of the Nineteenth Century; and yet it was so strange to Western ideas that the first foreign diplomats sent to Japan after the country was opened to the West could not understand it and did not know to whom to present their credentials. Yoritomo was the first Japanese statesman to realize that stabilized political power demanded that the direction of governmental affairs be removed from the shifting sway of the court and the intrigues of those who sought to use the Emperor for their own purposes. Occasionally, the Japanese Emperors had exercised governing power themselves; but usually, ministers and courtiers gained control and struggled about the Throne for their personal aggrandizement at the nation's cost. The Emperor was venerated by the people not as a political monarch but on a far higher level personifying centralized Heavenly spirit on earth. He was not, however, an ecclesiastical pope; he was the unified spiritual personality of the Japanese who regarded themselves as a united Shinto family descended from divinity in Heaven. The Ministers of State, being in attendance on the Emperor, artificially reflected somewhat the Throne's halo of austerity. They were able to isolate the Emperor for purposes of their own; and by concealing realities from him they succeeded in persuading him to crush loyal subjects, such as the famous scholar-statesman, Sugawara Michizane, who stood in their way by showing independent talent. The ministers did everything of importance in the Emperor's name. This system hampered effective criticism which is so necessary for progress. Governmental edicts, issued in reality by the ministers themselves, were given an authority as though coming directly from the Emperor. To criticize them or to oppose the ministers became, at times, almost treason, for the unique spiritual personality of the Emperor seemed to be involved. The Fujiwara family's misuse of its position so near to the Throne in order to elevate its influence to austere heights showed the peril of the system. Yoritomo met this situation in a way known only to genius. He removed the administrative capital from Kyoto, where the Emperor resided, to Kamakura, as far distant as he well could go. The Emperor, living in Kyoto, was not disturbed as the spiritual head of the nation. Kyoto became the spiritual capital of Japan while the political capital was maintained elsewhere. Thus, in modern terms, Yoritomo may be said to have separated State and Church in Japan many centuries before the West reached the same high level of evolution.

By this means, the Shogun became the responsible political director of the nation; and while his authority and position were very great, yet it was necessary for him to listen to advice and not ignore criticism so that rival politicians seeking power could be checked. To challenge the Shogun was very different from showing opposition to the Emperor. The Shogun could be, and was, on occasion overthrown without in any way threatening the continuity of the ruling dynasty of the Imperial Family. The Shogunate may well have saved Japan from the dynastic feuds so familiar in Western history. Opportunities were provided, through separation of Government from the Court, for talented leaders to compete for power without endangering the Throne even when political rivalries engendered long continued warfare. The battles were between local lords, not for or against the Emperor, but for or against the Shogun. The warring politicians could not use the Emperor's spiritual position to cloak their own materialistic ambitions. After the establishment of the Shogunate, the creative process can be discerned in Japan holding the national spirit co-ordinated in the Shinto personality of the Emperor, while individualism developed in the Shogunate field where political power was wielded. During generations of civil strife, the individualistic movement initiated by Yoritomo constantly widened, but cohesion was preserved spiritually through the Emperor, while the Japanese sensitiveness to utilitarian creative action encouraged materialistic co-ordination:

> The widespread warfare of the 14th century (in Japan) furthered rather than hindered domestic trade. The feudal commanders needed supplies for their troops and, if they were successful, for their domains. All this promoted the sale and the transport of commodities, and because the times were unsafe, merchants were obliged to cooperate in devising safeguards for their own interests. So there arose trade guilds and similar organizations, based often upon much earlier groupings, but now in a more perfected form. . . . The connection between these and religious institutions was very close and very ancient in origin. Traders would attach themselves to a monastery, ostensibly as purveyors of commodities for their own use, but in reality as a cover for other activities, in particular money-lending, because here they found the prestige of the church useful in enforcing payment of debts. . . . But those engaged in more legitimate trades also tended to form themselves into monopolistic groups under a patron. Thus, in Kyoto, the cotton clothiers' guild was composed of parishioners of the Gion Shrine, the yeast-brewers belonged to the Kitano Shrine and they relied upon these shrines to support them when they complained to the court or the *bakufu* (Shogunate) of any infringement of their privileges.[4]

---

[4] G. B. Sansom, Japan: A Short Cultural History, pp. 350-2.

Thus, new conditions of life engendered by civil strife stirred the creative activities of the Japanese, and the individualistic impetus expanded. New ideas of progress came forth because of the presence of the creative spirit within the nation. It was the creative spirit that turned even the destructive civil conflicts to good account by rising to meet the expanding environment. In mediaeval Europe at about the same time, the creative spirit was being similarly stimulated by the wars of the Crusades against the Moslems:

> The crusades contributed to the dissolution of feudalism by putting property on the market and disturbing the validity of titles; they aided the development of towns by vastly increasing the volume of trade; and they furthered the growth of scholasticism by bringing the West in contact with the mind of the East. . . . While a new spirit which compares and tolerates thus sprang from the crusades, the large sphere of new knowledge and new experience which they gave brought new material at once for scientific thought and poetic imagination. . . . The crusades afforded new details which might be inserted into old matters, and a new spirit which might be infused into old subjects.[5]

When Japan is criticized for absorbing new ideas from the West, it is well to remember that the West took new inspiration for both "scientific thought and poetic imagination" from the East, during the Crusades. Europe and Japan have the same creative competence to recognize new knowledge and expand their cultures when opportunities offer. Moslemism, however, did not learn from Europe during the Crusades and the rest of the Orient has not learned from Japan, and they have fallen. Mediaeval Europe, however, like mediaeval Japan, learned from adversity to rise higher under the inspiration of the creative spirit.

The mediaeval struggles in Japan elevated to supreme power three remarkable men: Oda Nobunaga, Toyotomi Hideyoshi and Tokugawa Iyeyasu. No other country ever has had at its service in any one period three leaders of such high abilities. Each had his own genius and each was highly individualistic and ambitious; but all acted together to curb the excess of individualistic political rivalries and unite the country— revealing through their different origins how the longing for co-operation as a progressive necessity had spread over Japan. Nobunaga was descended from a long line of Shinto officials; Hideyoshi's family was of poor peasant stock, and Iyeyasu belonged to the aristocratic Minamoto clan from which alone the Shoguns could be chosen. In them were

---

[5] Encyclopaedia Britannica, 14th Edition, article "Crusades," pp. 793-5.

symbolically united Shinto, the people and the nobility. It was this natural co-ordination of the national spirit that led through their efforts to the political consolidation of mediaeval Japan, giving peace to the country for nearly three hundred years, a longer period of internal and external concord than any other modern power has shown. The age of peace, however, did not destroy the virile spirit of Japan. Though the nation engaged in no conflicts from about the time of the death of Queen Elizabeth of England, yet when Japan was challenged with weapons new to her, nearly three centuries later, she was able to defeat China and then Russia because the Japanese people had not lost the impetus of creative action while China and Russia had passed under the influences of mechanism.

But, the Tokugawa Shogunate, which inherited the consolidation work of Nobunaga, Hideyoshi and Iyeyasu, at the beginning of the Seventeenth Century, tended toward over-confinement. The nation was closed to the world, and though the sacrifice was a practical measure of self-protection, yet the expansive activities of the people were not given opportunities adequate to their abilities. Wider reaches were needed. Individualism began to reassert itself in many ways. The Oyomei philosophy of practicality and personal responsibility grew in influence; and there was a revival of Pure Shinto in its phase of individual effort and spiritual co-ordination radiating from the Emperor.

The creative impetus found release when the West unlocked the doors of Japan from without. The Tokugawa Shogunate was overthrown and Shinto influences became politically supreme under constitutional government. The creative activities of the Japanese, individualized and co-ordinated afresh, moved forth from mediaevalism into the modern world, showing the same eager desires as in the past for new knowledge and new accomplishments, while retaining many aspects of the ancient ways of the race. So it is that Japan now reveals to the world a culture both ancestral and modern: strange flexibility of the creative impetus which perplexes the East as well as the West by its baffling manifestations of fluctuating standards struggling to reconcile primaeval subconscious intuitions with changing demands of modern self-conscious progress. Shinto provides the clue to interpreting this unique creative spirit of the Orient whose seeds were sown in the mythological age where the roots of Japanese culture still hold their original ground.

CHAPTER II

MYTHOLOGY AND CREATIVE BEGINNING

IN THE mythological age, primaeval man made humanity human. The slow evolution of mankind during the primitive eras of mental development was not a self-conscious movement. From the depths of subconsciousness the creative impetus provided the power that forced the advance despite all the perils and difficulties of progress. Life directed its own self-development from within itself. Mythological man subconsciously created co-ordinated activities, affection, family life, a sense of discipline, competence to adjust himself to changing conditions of existence, desire for the first tools and the skill to make them, reasoning processes of the mind and every other fundamental foundation on which modern progress rests. Language, the most important contribution humanity has made to life's mental progress, came into being in the mythological age.

None of these characteristics, marking the human race apart from other forms of life, arose by self-conscious effort. Primaeval man did not deliberately resolve to join with his fellows in common action, nor tell himself that he must invent new instruments for the hunt, nor inform his mind that it ought to take care of infancy through family love, nor did mythological humanity gather together and declare a united intention to create language. These developments arose as the subconscious impetus exerted its power on the surface of the mind. Direct intuitional knowledge that life has of itself was the controlling factor.

But, the subconscious direction could not have taken place if the creative impetus of life had not made itself into a material form equipped with organs designed for the purpose of giving expression to these desires. The moulding of the human body into the requisite organic form was likewise subconscious movement. Between life and matter there must be subjective co-ordination, implying a common fundamental source, or otherwise life could not turn matter into a living being. We know the subconscious impetus displays direct knowledge transcending the individual, for if this were not true adjustments between separated forms of life would be impossible. The most complex example of such knowledge is the adjustment between male and female for propagation of the species. Another striking example is the way the mother, after the birth of her child, develops milk for the child's nourishment exactly adjusted to the infant's digestive capacity. The mother gains no individual advantage by the change which takes place within herself. The advantage is accumulated by the infant. The mother does not self-consciously produce the milk for the child. It is the subconscious creative impetus of life that by this means assures life of survival. Life reveals in many other ways similar knowledge of itself as transcending the individual, while expressing this knowledge through the individual.

Vegetative nature, animal nature, human nature and Nature in all of its manifestations likewise show that the fundamental knowledge life has of itself and of materiality dwells in the subconscious, for it is by subjective direction that all existence is generated. Self-consciousness is a late comer in evolution. For many millions of years before life evolved self-consciousness, the subconscious mind of the universe slowly formed and changed its material manifestations.

The subconscious impetus, because of the way it has shown competence to mould life and matter during the long course of evolution, must be aware of subjective reality. It must have direct knowledge of life. Indeed, the subconscious creative impetus, we can say, actually is life's knowledge of itself and of materiality, self-evolving its own competence as it creates its own knowledge and makes that knowledge a part of itself, subjectively. The quality of consciousness, of self-conscious awareness of existence, is based on objectivity. Self-consciousness is the subconscious mind come to the surface to concentrate on objective action, so the direct subjective knowledge life has of itself cannot originate in the self-conscious:

> A reaction from the over-estimation of the quality of consciousness becomes the indispensable preliminary of any correct insight into the behavior of the psychic. In the words of Lipps, the unconscious must be accepted as the larger circle which includes within itself the smaller circle of the conscious: everything conscious has its preliminary step in the unconscious. . . . Its inner nature is just as unknown to us as is the reality of the external world and it is just as imperfectly reported to us through the data of consciousness as is the external world through the indications of our sensory organs.[1]

---

[1] Sigmund Freud, Interpretation of Dreams, pp. 486-7.

At times, poets, prophets and philosophers, and an occasional genius of science, move below the level of self-consciousness and gain insight into some aspect of subjective reality. After every such incursion, however, self-consciousness seeks surface examinations of the results as though jealous of its mental rights, causing confusions and perplexities to arise, for self-consciousness always wants to isolate results and bring objective experiences to bear on them. If self-consciousness were to negate its workings and "listen in," part of the truth dwelling in subconsciousness could arise to the surface. Since "everything conscious has its preliminary step in the unconscious," and since subconsciousness has given so many evidences of moving to the mind's surface in creating the foundations of civilization, it should be within the power of the subconscious impetus to send to the surface its direct knowledge of life, however inadequately self-consciousness may understand. Failure to know the inner nature of the subconscious mind does not prevent us from trying to understand what it says, any more than failure to know how the mind sends forth auditory impressions prevents us from listening to spoken words.

> It is not necessary to examine affairs with so much subtlety and so deep—a man loses himself in the consideration of so many contrary lustres and so many varied forms. . . . The best managers are those who can worst give account how they are so.[2]

To give account of how the subconscious mind conveys its knowledge to the mind's surface is as yet impossible. But, we know that it does so because we know self-consciousness does not direct life. Children are more subconscious in their mental processes than adults for they have not yet developed to any considerable extent their self-conscious mentalities:

> The child is incomparably superior to the average man in seeing the character of things. . . . This instinctive knowledge, the knowledge inherited from millions of past lives, is still fresh, not dulled by the weight of myriad impressions of education and personal experiences. Ask a child for example what he thinks of a certain stranger . . . and after long and painful effort he will suddenly come out with a comparison of startling truth that will surprise you, showing that he has perceived something in the face that you did not see.[3]

---

[2] Michel de Montaigne, Essays, translated by Charles Cotton, Vol. II, p. 399.

[3] Lafcadio Hearn, Life and Literature, chapter "On Composition," pp. 51-2.

During the childhood of the human race, direct instinctive knowledge, the subconscious knowledge that life has of itself, similarly gave to humanity insight into the character of things. Self-consciousness was but slightly developed and did not attempt in any extended way, to analyse the knowledge that came forth, and so destroy it. Among different races, the primaeval intuition of subjective reality emerged in different ways and at different periods; for the subconscious and self-conscious mental capacities of races differ greatly.

Some races tried to perpetuate the subconscious knowledge and in doing so, formed mythology. The primaeval myths of humanity are not the results of self-conscious efforts to analyse life. The age of analysis came very much later when self-consciousness was more highly evolved. Mythology is the outcome of subconscious knowledge rising to the surface. Humanity's initial intuitive understanding of life, the first information life gave about itself to humanity came forth in primitive myths. The mythology of the dead past, if we were able rightly to interpret its full meanings would give to us the living spirit of subconscious truth told to primitive man from within himself. The knowledge, however, is revealed in ways difficult for modern man to understand, for when self-consciousness revised parts of the myths, the direct meanings were not retained and when subconsciousness spoke with no self-conscious analytical intervention, the verbal expression became confused because primaeval man was not skilled in subtleties of language.

Nevertheless, because primaeval humanity clothed the sub-conscious truth in ill-assorted verbal garments is no reason for our refusal to acquaint ourselves with the offering. Novelists, dramatists and poets produce mythologies of the modern era, personalizing life's activities and forces of Nature often in distorted forms, just as did primaeval man. Romeo and Juliet are not actual beings but symbolize romantic love, representing it more accurately than any philosophic analysis. Faust talks like a living person but he is the speechless soul of man struggling in the objective world of desires. Tartuffe, Don Quixote, Nora, Beatrice and innumerable other personalized images of fiction and the stage are impersonal manifestations of psychological processes attired in modern mythological self-conscious dress. We call such works "fiction," but we know they are based on self-conscious reality. And, when we give a meaning of "fabrication" to mythology, we should understand that myths contain subconscious truth even though the creative processes are personalized instead of being analytically treated. Fiction, drama and poetry reflect the surface spirit of modern self-conscious reality; and though they utilize imaginary experiences that never happened to any single individual, and though they distort actuality, nevertheless they give accurate information concerning self-conscious reactions to life, Future historians will search them to discover the extent of our knowledge and what life meant to us, for the evidence is trustworthy. It confirms even to ourselves disquieting conclusions about self-consciousness:

> Our time is so utterly godless and profane, lacking as we do knowledge of the unconscious psyche and pursuing an exclusive cult of consciousness.[4]

Primaeval man was not godless nor profane. His subconscious psyche held him within the deep spiritual current of life and he could not pursue a cult of self-consciousness because his self-conscious mind was in the primary stage of evolution. Primaeval man was a self-conscious infant, but subconsciously and in his responses to intuitive knowledge he was more mature than modern man. The modern mythologies of poetry, fiction and the drama, show far higher language competence than do the mythologies of primitive man, and much more self-conscious analytical powers; but they do not reach to the subconscious depths, where knowledge of universal reality is concealed. Primaeval man communed with the depths but lacked the language ability. The mythologies of the primaeval past talk in spiritual terms about all existence, for the subconscious knowledge of the universe points that way. We speak of primitive "religion" but the ancient mythologies, when devoid of self-conscious sophistication are much broader in their conceptions than any religious doctrine, self-consciously formulated, ever has been:

> Primitive religion, though devoid of insight into its own deeper meaning, has a certain advantage over religion as an element in modern civilization, in that if less coherent, it is more comprehensive. All the values of life, utilitarian and humane, from food to sculpture and painting, from the study of plants and beasts to the study of the heavens, are primarily viewed by the savage as religious interests. After all, he lives in such a little world that he has in some ways a better chance of seeing the various institutions of society in their entirety as a way of life than can modern man, who to get a grip on his moral universe, must take so much more into consideration.[5]

---

[4] C. G. Jung, Commentary on Richard Wilhelm's Secret of the Golden Flower, p. 110.

[5] R. R. Marett, Rector of Exeter College, Oxford, Article "Anthropology" in Encyclopaedia Britannica, 14th Edition, Vol. II, p. 45.

The "deeper meanings" in the primaeval mind remain in the mythologies that primitive humanity has bequeathed to us. In studying them for the purpose of stating in modern terms what the fundamental implications seem to be, we are aided by the fortunate fact that science no longer can block the way. In the recent past, science would have scoffed at such a search and would have warned self-consciousness that its own efficiency could not be challenged by primitive knowledge of subconscious reality. Now, however, science is turning toward subjective explanations of life and matter due to its confusion over the revelations of its own investigators. Scientists are being compelled to abandon their former conviction that the test of reality must be based on objective experiments. Mathematical symbols are now sufficient to dissolve the universe; and physics and astronomy are wholly unable to state in coherent self-conscious language what their meanings really are. Their own verbal explanations are more confusing than the mythologies of primitive humanity. Science has contrite confessions to make. It is not objectivity but subjectivity that holds the key to unlock the door of life and the universe at large for our explorations of reality and the creative impetus. It is for the philosophic mind trained in subjective inquiry to find the way, helped however by the new science which sees other values in life than those based on objective materiality:

> The new teachings of astronomy and physical science are destined to produce an immense change in our outlook on the universe as a whole and on our views as to the significance of life. The question at issue is ultimately one for philosophic discussion, but before the philosophers have a right to speak, science ought first to be asked to tell all she can as to ascertained facts and provisional hypotheses.[6]

The facts and hypotheses of the new teachings of science are destroying the scientific myths which self-consciousness evolved through exclusive trust in objective knowledge. The theory of the indestructibility of matter, the doctrine of conservation of energy, the law of gravitation are no longer tenable. The material universe is being liberated from domination by omnipotent law. Indeterminacy, which means absence of absolutist control, is supplanting mechanism:

> The result of our analysis of physical phenomena up to the present is that we have nowhere found any evidence of the existence of determinism. . . . I do not think there is any obscurity as to the difference between deterministic and indeterministic types of law. Determinism

---

[6] Sir James Jeans, The Mysterious Universe, p. vii.

is usually understood to assert that there exist deterministic laws sufficient to deduce all future events from present existent data.[7]

That is to say, we inhabit a free universe, which is not controlled by Fate, but makes its own future. Even the earth and all the heavenly bodies go, in reality, anywhere they like:

> I hold to it that the earth goes anywhere it pleases. The next thing is that *we* must find out where it has pleased to go. The important question for us is not where the earth has got to in the inscrutable absolute behind the phenomena, but where we shall locate it in our conventional background of space and time. . . . The law of gravitation is not a stern ruler controlling the heavenly bodies; it is a kind-hearted accomplice who covers up their delinquencies.[8]

Self-consciousness can find no explanation for such a paradox. It is only in the subconscious spacelessness of the creative impetus that the answer eventually may be found. But, since modern science has discovered that the earth is not under omnipotent sway and can go anywhere it pleases, we can trust the truth of Shinto mythology which expresses the subconscious intuition that life is not dominated by omnipotence and also can go anywhere it pleases. If modern science now frees the heavenly bodies, Shinto freed the creative spirit itself, far back in primaeval times, by direct intuition of the knowledge life has of itself. Intuitional knowledge is knowledge of reality. If we turn for proof to philosophy, as science now authorizes us to do, we are told that:

> Intuitive knowledge has no need of a master, nor to lean upon any one; she does not need to borrow the eyes of others, for she has excellent eyes of her own. . . . If we imagine a human mind having intuitions for the first time, it would seem that it could have intuitions of actual reality, only. . . . But, where all is real, nothing is real. The child, with its difficulty of understanding true from false, history from fable, which are all one to childhood, can furnish us with a sort of very vague and only remotely approximate idea of this ingenuous state. Intuition is the undifferentiated unity of the real and the simple image of the possible.[9]

The child, like the primitive, though possessing intuitive knowledge, does accept fable for fact; but the intuitions come from within while the

---

[7] Sir Arthur Eddington, "Physics and Philosophy," in Philosophy, The Journal of the British Institute of Philosophy, January, 1933, pp. 38-40.

[8] Sir Arthur Eddington, The Nature of the Physical World, pp. 148-51.

[9] Benedetto Croce, Aesthetics, pp. 2-4.

confusions result because of inability to differentiate between fable and fact that arise on the surface of self-consciousness and become associated with the subconscious knowledge when it reaches the mind's surface. Primaeval man mixed the intuitive knowledge of the real originating in the subconscious with simple images of the possible, originating in self-consciousness. Not these self-conscious surface factors, but the subconscious intuitions, must guide us in seeking the primaeval truth of life's knowledge of itself buried in mythology. Modern anthropologists are beginning to realize the same basic fact in their studies of the customs of living primitives:

> It is a remarkable fact that the concepts which have been laboriously achieved by the students of conscious behaviour seem to have been of little avail hitherto in anthropology. . . . It cannot be doubted that the unconscious processes are of the greatest importance and interest to anthropologists.[10]

If the meanings of primitive ways of life cannot be found today on the self-conscious surface of the living primitive mind, but must be discovered in the subconscious, how can the surface wordings of myths provide an understanding of the primaeval knowledge of life without tracing them to their subconscious source? When myth makers engage in self-conscious attempts to explain life, the value of the myth always decreases. The Old Testament myth which describes Adam and Eve losing their innocence and being driven forth into the world of hardship and discord because they ate the forbidden fruit of knowledge, is based on true subconscious intuition. For, the creative impetus within life, forcing life away from belief in omnipotent control, to progress by self-effort, does encounter these obstacles. But the conclusion that the human race is born in sin because of this fact is an intrusion of self-consciousness seeking to explain the presence of "sin" in an assumed originally pure world. Such self-conscious expansions must be eliminated to reach the primaeval truth in mythology. The Old Testament myth of the creation of light, however, is an example of wholly uncontaminated subjective intuition. According to the Book of Genesis, Jehovah created light on the first day of creation but did not create the sun until the fourth day. That seems to self-conscious sophistication to be an absurdity; and no attempt is made in the myth to explain what is meant, for primaeval man did not know

---

[10] C. G. Seligman, Ánthropological Perspective and Psychological Theory," Journal of the Royal Anthropological Institute (London), July-December, 1932.

the meaning. The new science of our own time, however, offers a clue: for modern science is tending to believe that matter may be only radiation moving with less than the speed of light, while radiation may be only matter moving with the speed of light.

> These concepts reduce the whole universe to a world of light, potential or existent, so that the whole story of its creation can be told with perfect accuracy and completeness in the six words: "God said, 'Let there be light.'"[11]

These are the words of the Old Testament myth describing the creation of light on the first day. The unexplained creation of the sun three days after the creation of light, suggests that the subconscious mind in that early age, tried to express the idea that creation began with radiation, or, we may say, energy; but when the radiation idea reached the self-conscious surface of the mind, it became "light" though there was no light until the appearance of the sun. Yet, the myth was not grotesque in making light appear in the universe before the sun—for the meaning of subconsciousness was "potential light" or what, if modern science is right, we now call "matter." With such aids as this, supplied by modern scientific research, we may find clues concerning the direction to take in trying to probe the inner meanings of primaeval mythology. We must try to enter the racial subconsciousness as far as we can, through our own mental depths, much as Bergson shows that by first familiarizing ourselves with surface manifestations and then sinking ourselves into the stream of life, we can observe reality. We must, likewise, try to study the primaeval mentality through knowledge of the activities of the primal humans who made the myths and followed the traditions created by the myths. This is an invaluable guide; for though primaeval man did not understand the subconscious truth in any logical, coherent, way, nevertheless he responded to subconscious knowledge in terms of direct action. It is by activities far more than by words that even modern man expresses his attitudes toward life; and primaeval man, who was verbally immature, manifested his conceptions almost entirely by his reactions to the subconscious knowledge life has of itself.

The more a mythology is founded on subconsciousness and the less it has been influenced by self-consciousness, the less do artificial and changing conditions of existence confuse the meanings which the intuition of life seeks to express. Myths may, however, exert degenerative influences.

---

[11] Sir James Jeans, op. cit., pp. 83-4.

For, if versatility of action ceases in any culture and the ancient mythology remains, its implications are misinterpreted and its form is changed causing superstitions and other obnoxious substitutes for creative action to arise. For man to progress he must move out of the simplicity of the primaeval age, and in general the self-conscious development which ensues causes the old mythology gradually to disappear. If, however, a culture can become progressive and at the same time carry with it the primaeval racial traditions, uncontaminated by self-consciousness, then an invaluable opportunity for exploring the subconscious truth is presented to us.

Such is the case with the mythology of Shinto, which in this respect occupies a special position in mythological lore. Shinto myths are nearer to pure subconscious intuition than are any other primitive traditions that modern man has inherited, for the Japanese have held fast to their racial sub-consciousness far longer than any other modern nation has done. Primaeval Shinto, consequently has been carried into modern times, neither perverted by self-consciousness nor become degenerative through inaction. The cultures of India, China and the West grew from within each cultural unit by self-conscious expansion which submerged the subconscious under pressure of surface analysis and logic. Japan, however, did not so assiduously apply self-consciousness in the nation's evolutionary development. The results of sophisticated self-consciousness reached the Japanese mind from India, China and the West. The Japanese absorbed and modified these offerings and made them part of the Japanese spirit very largely by the subconscious processes of the creative impetus. Japanese subconsciousness, therefore, was not suppressed by self-consciousness which has not developed itself in Japan with the same intensity as in other great cultures. Even today, the Japanese respond more to inner feelings than to self-conscious analysis. Their intense competence for creative activity is more a subconscious process than in the West where self-consciousness is supreme. Shinto mythology, therefore, is unique in that it has continued a vital force in Japan from mythological to modern times, and so offers a field of its own for studying the truth about life as known to primaeval humanity.

The very fact that Shinto underwent a strong revival in Japan coincident with the emergence of Japanese culture from mediaeval to modern ways of progress shows it must possess qualities of creative influence within its mythology. Other mythologies have receded before the tide of progress. Shinto is strengthened by material progress; for in the Shinto myths life shows direct subjective knowledge of itself and the universe. But, Shinto mythology is difficult to understand, spiritually, because the primaeval compilers were so completely responsive to the intuition that not only life but all materiality is divine spirit. Tennyson wrote that if we could understand the flower in the crannied wall, all in all, we would know what man and God is, implying all life is divine spirit; but Shinto includes the crannied wall, as well, in the divine identity. There is further difficulty in comprehending Shinto myths because they confuse vaguely remembered racial historical events with imagined Heavenly happenings, and use both to personalize pure subconscious knowledge of reality. Fortunately, however, there is no attempt at self-conscious analysis nor any effort to be logically convincing; for had self-consciousness attempted either of these expedients to make the myths "read well," the subconscious truth would have disappeared in the process. The primaeval Shinto mentality had no developed expository apparatus, and while coherence suffered, the subconscious truth remained undisturbed within its tangled verbal wrapping.

The history of Japan, according to Shinto mythology, began before there was a Japan. Its commencement was in Heaven, not, however, as a theological dogma, but in keeping with the subconscious Shinto intuition that all life and all materiality are emergences of divine creative spirit into objectivity. Shinto calls Heaven, *Takama-no-Hara*, which means "The Plain of High Heaven." But, in this term, as in the Shinto conception of the history of Japan beginning in Heaven, two ideas are present, which became confused in the primaeval mind. The primitive racial memory must have known that the Japanese originated in lands far from Japan, perhaps in southern islands and on the northern Asiatic mainland as well. It is not unusual for colonists to idealize their original home and call it Heaven, however imperfect it may have been. So *Takama-no-Hara* suggests a spatial abode, whereas Shinto really emphasizes the spacelessness of spirituality more than do formal religions, for Shinto uses neither statues nor pictures to represent divine spirit or Heaven at Shinto Shrines. The true Shinto conception of Heaven is not a spatial part of the universe, but spacelessness or subjectivity. The Shinto mythology, in representing Japan as having its historical origin in Heaven, therefore, was idealizing the dimly remembered racial homeland, and was using this memory to localize and thereby increase the vividness of the truth that the entire universe is divine spirit. This profound subconscious knowledge of reality is what the primaeval mentality tried to express and is the fundamental part of the myth that has exerted a profound and lasting influence on Japanese culture. In this sense, the history of Japan, as of the universe at large did begin in Heaven, the originating subjective center of divine creative spirit expanding objectively. We cannot dismiss such a conception as the outcome of primitive ignorance and imaginings, for modern man is beginning to turn self-consciously to the same understanding under the influence of the new discoveries of science that the universe is non-material in origin. If it is non-material, the original source must be subjective, not objective, and if we wish to give to the fount of subjective creativeness coming forth as the material universe the name of Heaven, science can offer no effective objection nor any alternative.

In Shinto there is no separation between the universe and divine creative spirit. The universe is divine creative spirit extending itself as matter and as life. There are not three entities: spirit, matter and life. Matter and life are divine spirit self-creating itself in different manifestations but always divine spirit. So, no dualism exists in Shinto, and the monistic conception toward which modern science is now tending, indicates how loyal to the subconscious knowledge of reality Shinto mythology has remained, despite its lack of verbal expression. Indeed, it was the very incoherence of primaeval man that permitted the subconscious truth to rise to the surface where it remained so largely undisturbed by self-consciousness. When the Shinto mythology was being formulated, the Japanese had no self-conscious culture to contaminate subconscious truth:

> They had no tea, no fans, no porcelain, no lacquer—none of the things in fact, by which in later times they have become chiefly known. They did not yet use vehicles of any kind. They had no accurate method of computing time, no money, scarcely any knowledge of medicine. Neither, though they possessed some sort of music and poems, a few of which at least are not without merit, do we hear anything of the art of drawing. But the most important art of which they were ignorant is that of writing.[12]

Had Professor Chamberlain but known it, this description does not vitiate Shinto. It is testimony, instead, to the lack of self-consciousness which allowed the subconscious intuition of reality to consolidate itself as a permanent influence in Japan. Nor did foreign influences intrude to undermine the directness of the racial understanding of life:

---

[12] B. H. Chamberlain, Introduction to his translation of the Kojiki, 2nd edition, p. xlviii.

The old Shinto owes little to any outside source. It is on the whole an independent development of Japanese thought.[13] Shinto is Japanese in the way the myths are recounted. It is Japanese, too, in the fact that only in Japan has the primaeval subconscious intuition that the universe and divine creative spirit are the same been preserved as an integral part of national life. But, Shinto is more than this. Shinto is more than Japanese in that it is an expression of living reality, not a limited experience but life in its broadest sense. It expresses life's knowledge of itself in the form of a national history, but the meaning is world-wide in its applicability. Humanity, in general, must have had subconscious knowledge of reality similar to Shinto's fundamental implications, for there are traces of the same conception in other mythologies, though the knowledge was expressed more indirectly and has undergone innumerable changes either because of debasements or because self-consciousness has tried to modify the subconscious truth and interpret it in accordance with defective surface studies of life and materiality.

It is common for the same primal intuition, springing from humanity's subconscious knowledge of life, to have the direct, basic meaning retained by one culture and lost by another. Thus, in Chinese and Japanese, the word *tennen* means "Nature" and also "made by Heaven," so that in both languages, the same sentence reads: "Nature is blooming" and "Heaven is blooming." The word *shizen,* which is likewise the same in Chinese and Japanese, is another term for "Nature" and means also, "spontaneously made." Primaeval China must have understood the fundamental significance of these words in their related meanings, but the Chinese developed a sophisticated and self-conscious mentality, submerging the original subconscious intuition. So, the Chinese lost the profound implications of the identity of "Nature," "made by Heaven" and "spontaneously made."

In Japan, however, where self-conscious logic never has dominated the mind to the exclusion of subconscious understandings, the basic purport of the association of the three terms never has been lost by Shinto. In the Shinto mythology, Nature is made by Heaven spontaneously; that is to say, Nature actually is Heaven self-creating itself objectively. Nature is not a mechanical product of an aloof manufacturing principle in Heaven; Nature is Heaven or divine spirit, itself, self-expanding. So, in

---

[13] W. G. Aston, Shinto (in Religions Ancient and Modern Series), p. 3.

this direct meaning of the words *tennen* and *shizen,* when Nature is bloom-ing, it is Heaven that is blooming; and in the same sense, Nature and "spontaneously made" can mean the same thing with perfect consist-ency.

It was natural for Japan to take from China the words *tennen* and *shizen* in their original meanings because Shinto had always followed the same understanding of the universe, and no revaluation of the terms was necessary in Japan, although the original significance had disap-peared in China where only lip service was paid to it. After Japan was opened to Chinese influences, many such expressions were adopted by the Japanese, whose ancient purport had lost vitality and become mecha-nized on the continent. The primary ideas, however, were understood by the Japanese in their literal sense, due to the power of subconsciousness in Japanese culture and the pure knowledge of life that Shinto had im-planted in Japanese tradition. When, therefore, Chinese ways of expression are found in Shinto, the meaning is not that. Shinto owes its conceptions of reality to China. The Chinese made some of the words but had lost the right understanding of them due to many centuries' wor-ship of logic and the elevation of knowledge bereft of action to supremacy in their culture. The Japanese, from the beginning of their history, had struggled to remain loyal to the primaeval subconscious understanding of reality without verbally expressing the ideas; and so Shinto found some Chinese terms, in their original meanings, suitable for adoption, when Chinese self-expression had become familiar to the Japanese. It is necessary to take such wordings in their literal sense, not as figures of speech, in order to understand the Shinto conceptions, for they entered into the Japanese language, not in imitation of Chinese thought but be-cause they were understood according to the subconscious intuition of Shinto.

In one of her illuminating sentences that make Tenth Century Japan seem so modern in its understanding of human nature, Murasaki Shikibu said: "Often one cannot recognize qualities simply because one does not expect them to be there."[14] This is especially true of the modern attitude toward the primaeval subconscious mind of humanity. We do not expect fundamental knowledge of life to have been there and so we cannot rec-ognize the basic conceptions that are buried in Shinto mythology. Even when the subconscious implications are clarified by study of the words

---

[14] Genji, Arthur Waley's translation, Vol. V, p. 35.

and the cultural consequences, we are tempted to remain skeptical, declaring the interpretations are artificial or strained, so persistently has the modern mind come to regard self-consciousness as the fount of all knowledge.

However, with philosophy and science in recent decades turning toward spontaneity of creativeness as the generating source of the universe, it is becoming increasingly difficult to decry the subconscious insight of primaeval man, as expressed in Shinto, for the implication of creative spontaneity runs throughout Shinto mythology. The expressions are not in philosophic or scientific terms, but they are as descriptive of the process of creativeness as early man was able to make them. The fact that subconsciousness did not express all that it was struggling to say in Shinto does not mean the compilers of the tradition were more incompetent, relative to their era, than are modern writers:

> An author may know pretty nearly all that he *has said,* but it is quite certain, however paradoxical it may sound, that he never knows very welt all that his mind has been struggling *to say,* or to put it more precisely, all that his work means to convey, in all its significance, whither and how far it points.[15]

Here is evidence from one of the leading modern philosophers, that the mind struggles to send to the surface inner meanings that never are fully expressed. Yet, examination by others often reveals significances that the author has not self-consciously realized. So it is with the Shinto mythology. Primaeval man struggled to make known the subconscious knowledge that life has of itself, but had not the words to objectify the subconscious truth, nor did he fully realize self-consciously all that the innermost intuition sought to clarify. Yet enough emerged for the basic implications to be understood if the wordings are adequately examined. Thus in the original preface to the Kojiki, the oldest compilation of Shinto tradition, written in 712 A.D., the author summarizes the contents of the book and gives the following description of the commencement of creation:

> Now when Chaos had begun to condense, but force and form were not yet manifest, and there was nought named, nought done, who could know its shape? Nevertheless, Heaven and Earth first parted and the Three Deities (Kami) performed the commencement of creation.[16]

---

[15] Jacques Chevalier, Henri Bergson, p. 75.

[16] B. H. Chamberlain's translation, 2nd edition, p. 4.

"Chaos" usually means disorder or confusion; but since there was no force or form, there was no power to produce disorder and there were no things to get into confusion. Nor can Chaos have meant nothingness, for as Bergson has shown,[17] nothingness, in a material sense, implies always the absence of something previously existing. No-thing means a thing that was but has disappeared. The true sense of Chaos in Shinto, as meaning existence precedent to force and form, is subjectivity. Chaos beginning to condense must be regarded in Shinto as subjectivity or spacelessness becoming self-creativity objective. Everybody has daily experience of subjectivity expanding into objectivity. Ideas within the mind are subjective or spaceless; but when an idea begins to condense and comes forth as words, it becomes objective or spatial. If the words were self-developing after becoming objective—as indeed they may be in their influence on others—then we would have an example of the Shinto conception of pure creativeness expanding from subjectivity into objectivity: continuing to be, objectively, all the new meanings that the words develop, while also being, subjectively, more than the words and able to expand as other words or actions. Since modern science shows electrons are motion or energy without material form, so there may be Pure Thought or Pure Mind without a thinker, until the thinker is evolved for the subjective idea to become objective.

The Shinto description of the commencement of creation is dominated by the subconscious idea of creative spontaneity. There can be no principle of mechanism in the conception that when force and form were not yet manifest the shape of what was to ensue—the future content of the universe—could not be known. Absolutist omnipotence or mechanism must know in advance of the use of force or form what the eventual shape will be. Since there was no such advance knowledge, it is clearly indicated how Shinto tradition, at the very beginning, moved away from omnipotent mechanism toward the idea of creativeness.

The word "Deities" in the original is "Kami," a Shinto expression meaning divine spirit,[18] personalized individualistically. The Kojiki states the first three Kami "became alone, and hid their persons,"[19] meaning

---

[17] *Creative Evolution*, translated by Arthur Mitchell, pp. 276 et seq.

[18] See the author's analysis of the word "Kami" in Chapter III.

[19] B. H. Chamberlain's translation, 2nd edition, p. 17.

they were self-creative and vanished after performing the commencement of creation. There is no description of a universe being made
mechanically at the commencement of creation. The three Kami initiated the creative impetus, that is all; and this conception is consistently
followed in Shinto mythology, for in the succeeding parts of the myths
Kami or divine spirit creates itself, or expands objectively, as the manifestations of life and matter.

The first Kami, Ame-no-mi-naka-nushi-no-Kami, the Center of Heaven
Kami, does not return to the records, after his first disappearance. In
him, the emphasis falls with intuitional force on the idea of "commencement as the creative impetus, initiating itself and thereafter
self-developing, not being subjected to an omnipotent center of Heaven
mechanism. In Shinto, there is no Heavenly center directing the course
of the universe. The universe, itself, is Heaven, objectified, and self-
creating its future.

The two other Kami who performed the commencement of creation,
reappear later in the records after the first disappearance. They are called
Taka-mi-musubi-no-Kami, High-August-Producing Kami and Kami-
musubi-no-Kami, Divine-Producing Kami. The essential word in their
names is *musubi*, which means "producing" in the sense of growth as an
indwelling creative impetus. These two personalizations of divine spirit
are frequently designated as the Producing Kami or the Kami of Growth.
Sometimes they are interpreted as representing but one fundamental
conception—growth. There is a sense in which this is true, for all growth
in the universe is the self-development of divine spirit or Kami; but in
individualizing the two movements of growth, it seems probable that
there was an effort to distinguish between growth in its vegetative aspect
and growth in its mental expansion.

Kami-musubi-no-Kami in a later part of the mythology becomes the
impetus that causes grain to grow from seeds. His son, Sukuna-biko-na-
no-Kami, descends to earth and jointly with Okuninushi, consolidates
the land. The son's identity was revealed by Kuye-biko, who after the
son's disappearance from earth, became known as "the scarecrow in the
mountain fields."[20] Here is an attempt to emphasize that consolidation
means not only creative human effort—through Okuninushi— but also
the creative impetus growing the grains in the ground. The association
of the scarecrow with the grains has an obvious significance. The

---

[20] Kojiki, B. H. Chamberlain's translation, 2nd edition, pp. 102-5.

mythology says the scarecrow "knows everything in the Empire," implying the primaeval Japanese, like other peoples, believed birds know everybody's secrets, and presumably whispered everything to the scarecrow. Even today, in the West, people say "a little bird told me," when not wishing to divulge the identity of an informant.

The second Kami of Growth, Taka-mi-musubi-no-Kami, becomes in the mythology, the associate of Amaterasu-o-mi-Kami, the Ruler of Heaven, and is called Taka-gi-no-Kami, "High-Integrating" Kami. The basic idea in the primaeval mind that struggled here for expression is shown in the name of his son, Omoi-kane-no-Kami, the "Thought-Includer" Kami, who "included in his single mind the thoughts and contrivances of many."[21] The more accurate interpretation of his name would thus be "Thought-Co-ordinator." He is the mythological adviser to the other Kami, personifying mental co-ordination as an entity in itself, somewhat as modern *Gestalt* psychology maintains that the co-ordinated whole is more than the sum of the parts.

Thus, the three Kami who "performed the commencement of creation" symbolize in different ways the creative divine spirit, self-developing. The Center of Heaven Kami, disappearing entirely after the "commencement," represents the creative impetus not being controlled mechanically. The first Kami of Growth symbolizes the creation of vegetation, and the second Kami of Growth represents individual mental integration and its creative expansion as co-ordinated mentally. Following the appearance of the three original creative Kami, the mythology names other Kami

> who were generated spontaneously independently from one another. All of them came out of the primaeval chaos and vanished without a trace. However, their titles indicate that they were intended to personify powers of spontaneous generation, such as mud, vapour, germs were thought to be.[22]

The idea of divine spirit self-creatively expanding was thus emphasized still further in the Shinto conception of the commencement of material existence. Two other Kami thereafter appear, Izana-gi-no-Kami, the Male-Who-Invites, and Izana-mi-no-Kami, the Female-Who-Invites. They are the Adam and Eve of Shinto mythology, the first of the Heavenly Kami

---

[21] Motoori Norinaga, quoted by B. H. Chamberlain in his translation of the Kojiki, 2nd edition, p. 65, note 7.

[22] Masaharu Anesaki, History of Japanese Religion, p. 25.

who procreate sexually, although later, the Male-Who-Invites procreates alone. Differences in ways of procreation are marked in Shinto mythology, an indication of the extreme simplicity of self-consciousness in the primaeval mind when the Shinto tradition was being formed. The confusion is natural in primitive times, for fatherhood was unknown to early man. There are still tribes in Africa and Australia who do not know the husband is the father of the child: it is believed motherhood results by a totem spirit entering the woman. The discovery of paternity was a momentous triumph of human thought and led to a spiritual conception of the man's part in producing the child, which gave rise to phallicism. Phallic observances in Shinto are not indications of sensuality but are forms of paying respect to the spiritual mystery of life begetting off-spring through the male.

In early Japanese culture, the mother entered a confinement hut alone for the birth of her child. The custom must have originated when paternity was unknown and it was thought necessary to isolate the woman from earthly relationships when her child, supposedly generated by unseen spirit, was to appear. After knowledge of fatherhood was acquired, the ancient tradition doubtless had become so firmly fixed as a spiritual rite that it could not be broken; and the custom continued in some parts of Japan into the Meiji era—a demonstration of the tenacious hold tradition has on Japanese culture.

> A social system is kept together by the blind forces of instinctive action and instinctive emotions clustered around habits and prejudices. It is, therefore, not true that any advance in the scale of culture inevitably tends to the preservation of Society. On the whole, the contrary is more often the case, and any survey of nature confirms this conclusion. A new element in life renders in many ways the operation of the old instincts unsuitable. But, unexpressed instincts are unanalyzed and blindly felt. Disruptive forces, introduced by a higher level of existence, are then warring in the dark against an invisible enemy. . . . Those societies which cannot combine reverence to their symbols with freedom of revision must ultimately decay either from anarchy or from the slow atrophy of a life stifled by useless shadows.[23]

This is modern Japan's position today. New elements have entered the national life and the old instincts are warring in the dark and are being questioned. But, the ancient symbols remain, and though modern knowledge offers ways of revision, yet the revisions must not cause

---

[23] A. N. Whitehead, Symbolism, Its Meaning and Effect, pp. 68-9, 88.

changes in basic meanings. Rather, the mythology of Shinto can be reinterpreted to restore the primaeval truth of life in keeping with the new understanding of modern progress, as a fresh inspiration for creative action. To make self-consciousness aware of the buried subconscious truths of Shinto will dispel the disruptive forces and clarify the unanalyzed and blindly felt instincts warring in the dark of the mind, so that the modern spirit of Japan and the nation's ancient culture shall continue to remain co-ordinated.

CHAPTER III

THE MEANING OF SHINTO

BEFORE Japan had established intellectual contact with the Asiatic continent, the spiritual belief of the people had no name. It naturally would have none because the Japanese did not differentiate between the human and the divine. The way of life was regarded as the way of Kami, the spirit of Heaven extended into the material universe, and no other way was considered to exist. Thus, the word for government in Japanese is *matsuri-goto*. *Matsuri* is a shrine observance or celebration, and *goto* means "thing." Government thus means "shrine observance thing" or "attending to Kami affairs." The meaning is not that Heaven directs earthly activities but that man is Heavenly spirit on earth.

It is difficult to understand the profound significance of this fact, for we customarily think of man and spirit as not being the same. It seems so necessary to give specific names to spiritual doctrines that when we encounter a direct subconscious intuition in Shinto which regards all human activities, good or bad, as spiritual or Kami actions, we imagine a lack of primitive competence to understand life. On the contrary, the absence of a name for the primaeval Japanese spiritual conception implies the immediacy of the truth, for it means all life and the entire universe are spirit: a conception which modern man increasingly is striving to comprehend.

It is true that spirituality must be defined when man seeks to understand himself and the universe in self-conscious, analytical terms as being other than material or mechanical. But, not until self-consciousness knows—as it is now beginning to know—that materiality originates in the immaterial, can the self-conscious mind be trusted to comprehend that life, too, has its origin in subjectivity of spirit and not in objective matter. Subconscious intuition seems always to have known that both life and materiality have a non-material source, which we express as spirit; and the Japanese in the primaeval age emphasized in the mythology of Shinto this element of the subconscious knowledge that life has of reality. The very keenness of the Japanese subconscious mind kept the nation self-consciously naive, unsophisticated and racially unanalytical, though sustaining at the same time the impetus of creative action and the power of discipline. The Japanese explored the minds of others, but seldom their own minds, developing a culture of subconscious intensity that tended to check self-conscious expression.

On the continent of Asia, however, self-conscious sophistication was acquired very early and it largely suppressed direct responses to primaeval intuitions. Interest in analysis for its own sake spread and replaced desire for action. The Chinese adopted the formula "knowledge is easy but action is difficult," and told themselves that the wise man, therefore, turns from action to knowledge.[1] When continental sophistication reached Japan, it became necessary to differentiate such ideas from the Japanese conception of life. How this was done we do not know. The Manyo-shu, the first collection of Japanese poems, contains a contribution by Hitomaru Kakinomoto, the greatest poet of the Seventh Century, the era of Chinese cultural inundation of Japan, which says: "Japan is the land where people do not like surface discussion so much." There can have been little discussion of spiritual principles among the early Japanese; and it is necessary to go below the surface meanings of the words in order to understand their full significance.

Shinto did not come into use immediately to differentiate Japanese from Chinese conceptions. The original expression was Kami Nagara. Nagara means "natural" or "the same as" or "from." If a culture were called "Matter Nagara," the meaning clearly would be "natural matter" or "the same as matter" or "from (in the sense of originating from) matter," implying "whatever is, is matter," indicating a materialistic conception of life. In the same sense, Kami Nagara can mean "whatever is, is Kami," (or divine spirit). Kami Nagara has been interpreted as "Kami-like"; but this expression may imply that man must strive to be like Kami or man is naturally pure as Kami may be conceived as being. These are not meanings found in Shinto mythology, however, for the inherent Shinto idea is that everything, whatever its nature, good or bad, is Kami-like.

Later, the Chinese word Shinto found general use. The Japanese pronunciation of the Chinese ideographs for Shinto is Kami no Michi; and it is necessary to examine both pronunciations in order to discover the

---

[1] Professor Hu Shih supplied this information to the author.

full meanings. The syllable *mi* in "Michi" is a Heavenly title, "august" or "divine."[2] *Chi* is a very old Japanese word for "way." Michi thus means "divine way," and Kami no Michi or Shinto is often interpreted as "the Kami divine Way" or "Kami-ism." Further elucidation, however, is necessary to understand what the primaeval Japanese mentality sought to express.

The syllable *to* in Shinto was derived from *Tao*, the term used for the Chinese doctrine of Lao-Tze. The ancient Chinese ideograph for *Tao* was a cross-road with hairs in the centre representing the severed head of a criminal—the hairs simply clarifying the ideograph as meaning a cross-road, for heads of criminals were commonly exposed at Chinese cross-roads. Later the ideograph was changed and *Tao* was made into two characters. One means hair, presumably to retain the original idea of the cross-road, and the other means head, implying a human head. The two characters thus can mean "man at the cross-road" or "man facing the universe" with the indication that at the cross-road man chooses his own way or observes life. These two characters represent the syllable to in Shinto. The Japanese added to *to* the Chinese word *Shin*, meaning Kami; and by pronouncing *to* as *michi*, they also added the idea of "divine" to the cross-road. So Shinto can mean: Kami man (or man as Kami) at the divine cross-road choosing his way. The "divine" cross-road means all the universe is divine spirit.

There is a fundamental difference between Taoism and Shinto in man's choice at the cross-road. In Taoism, the sage chooses to contemplate life passively, seeking supreme virtue without effort, and denying spiritual values to life. Taoism's extreme example of inaction is fear even of doing good, expressed by Yang Chu (Yang-tse), twenty-five hundred years ago:

> You may do good without thinking about fame, but fame will come to you nevertheless. You may have fame without aiming at pelf, but pelf is sure to follow in its wake. You may be rich without wishing to provoke emulation and strife, yet emulation and strife will certainly result. Hence, the superior man is very cautious about doing good.[3]

To this demoralizing extreme China's interest in logic and analysis as an intellectualistic game had carried continental leaders of thought a

---

2 It is translated as "divine" by Genchi Kato and Hikoshiro Hoshiro in Kogoshui, 3rd edition, p. 68, critical note 46.

3 Lionel Giles, Taoist Teachings, p. 118.

thousand years before Chinese culture entered Japan. During that period Japan had struggled to develop creative action, and Shinto conceives the cross-road as an opportunity to advance in search of progress, not to sit down idly contemplating existence.

At the cross-road, or in the universe, man as Kami moves forward, dynamically. The word "Kami" however, must be examined to show the meaning. Kami is usually translated as God or gods; but the idea of deity creating or guarding mankind is absent from Shinto. Kami has an earthly and a Heavenly meaning, showing in this way that Shinto does not separate the human and the divine. Kami literally means superior; and it is used to designate a person of superior position or the superior—top—part of the body, the head and hair. Kami as "superior" cannot be applied to one person as being actually superior to another, for in Shinto everybody is Kami. It is the person's superior material position that permits the title of Kami. The basic meaning of Kami, in its spiritual sense, is that everybody is superior in position through having a Heavenly origin. Heaven is commonly regarded as above or superior to the earth. So, Kami as "superior" as a generalized spiritual term really means "Heavenly being" or in modern terms "divine spirit."

Further indication that Kami embraces the conception of divine spirit is shown by the common use in Shinto mythology of the expression *mitama*, which means august or divine jewel or spirit, and is applied to the Kami. The Kami are explained in Shinto as having Ara-Mitama, "Rough Divine Spirit," the spirit of creative action, and Nigi-Mitama, "Gentle Divine Spirit," the balancing counterpart. Motoori Norinaga warns against the mistaken idea that some Kami are Ara-Mitama and others Nigi-Mitama, and he asserts they are different manifestations of the same spirit.[4] W. G. Aston states that "Spirit is the nearest English equivalent for *mitama*. . . . The old records rarely distinguish between the God's (Kami's) real body and his *mitama*", and he quotes Hirata Atsutane as saying the Kojiki and Nihongi the two earliest books of Shinto mythology, do not differentiate between the *Utsushi-mi-mi*, the Real Divine Body and the *mitama*, the Divine Spirit of the Kami.[5] Japanese and foreign commentators thus unite in showing that *mitama* means august or divine spirit and that Shinto does not differentiate between Kami body and divine spirit: so Kami and divine spirit are the same.

[4] B. H. Chamberlain's translation of the Kojiki, 2nd edition, p. 282, note 9.

[5] Shinto: The Way of the Gods, pp. 26, 31, 34.

Hence, the indicated meaning of Shinto or Kami no Michi becomes: Man is divine spirit at the divine cross-road or in the divine universe, choosing his way. To understand the full content of the primaeval spiritual conception, however, Kami Nagara should be united to Kami no Michi, as Kami Nagara no Michi. The complete primaeval intuition then appears: Whatever is, is divine spirit; man is divine spirit in the divine universe choosing his way. This is the subconscious truth of life's knowledge of reality that primaeval man sought to express in Shinto.

Divine spirit, however, in Shinto, does not mean theological omnipotent divinity. Divine spirit in Shinto is the universe in every aspect, seeking self-creative growth, with freedom of choice. So, divine spirit can take the wrong road as well as the right, and can sacrifice itself to its own eventual progress. Whatever the result, good or bad, Kami is always Kami: divine spirit can never lose its divinity.

Kami Nagara, "whatever is, is divine spirit," is not a philosophic phrase nor a mystical idea without practical reality in Shinto. The woodlands, the flowers of the field, crops in their seasons, the dust of the road and the water that lays the dust and the germs of disease in the dust, animal life and humanity, beneficial or harmful, are all divine spirit. Fire, mountains, seas, every material as well as every living form of the universe Is Kami or divine spirit. Shinto does not mean Nature was made by divine spirit, for to Shinto there are not two entities, divine spirit and Nature. Nature *is* divine spirit come forth from subjectivity as the objective universe. Mountains and seas do not have spirits dwelling in them. Everything *is* divine spirit, for there are many ways for the Kami creative spirit to express itself. Thus Motoori Norinaga says:

> There are many cases of seas and mountains being called Kami. It is not their spirits which are meant. The word was applied directly to the seas or mountains themselves as being very awful things.[6]

Hirata Atsutane says the same, adding that the word Kami was used directly "of the sea on account of its depth and the difficulty of crossing it; of the mountain on account of its loftiness."[7] Here, however, is an instance of self-consciousness attempting to add to the mythological intuition, for shallow waters and low hills are likewise Kami in Shinto. No reason is given in the mythology itself for Kami becoming mountains,

---

[6] W. G. Aston, op. cit., pp. 8-9.

[7] Sir Ernest Satow, Revival of Pure Shinto in appendix to Vol. III, Transactions of the Asiatic Society of Japan.

seas and all Nature. To primaeval man, no reason was necessary for he accepted without any reservation the intuitive truth that the entire universe is Kami or divine spirit. Motoori and Hirata, however, though possessing much critical ability, wrote in the Eighteenth Century during a time when effort was being made to elevate Shinto above foreign influences in Japanese self-consciousness. They considered it necessary to attempt to clarify the Shinto obscurities, and while they succeeded in part, they occasionally were led astray by seeking only surface meanings. They interpreted Kami too literally to mean superior or powerful, in terms of height and depth and awe-inspiring. These subordinate surface meanings give false clues, for in Shinto, everybody and everything, high and low, weak and strong, are all Kami. The pure intuition of primaeval man was that mountains and seas are not dwelling places of Kami or divine spirit, but actually are themselves Kami. They were not made by Kami or divine spirit, they are Kami itself become objectified. Primaeval man did not explain how or why but recounted the simple, direct fact. The directness of the subconscious intuition is indicated by the fact that the primaeval mentality escaped the dilemma of dualism; for if spirit dwells in the sea or mountain, a dualistic conception is involved, while if the sea or mountain is itself actual spirit, a monistic interpretation is inevitable.

Until a few years ago, modern science would have dismissed this idea as an indication of primitive ignorance and defective imagination; but no longer is that possible. Fundamentally, primaeval man was right, according to the most recent tendencies of Western science. Primaeval man's vocabulary was limited, however, and his low self-conscious explanatory abilities were unable to clarify the meaning. Nevertheless, the meaning was sufficient to him to guide his activities and attitudes, and that is the final test of meanings. Modern science comes close to the Shinto principle that Nature has no origin of its own, in any material sense, but is Kami or divine spirit, for science has demolished materialism. Neither the seas nor the mountains nor any other part of the universe has fundamental material reality of its own, according to the new physics. Science does not use the word "Kami" to explain the universe, but uses the words "thought" or "mind." The difference is one of terminology more than of principle. Primaeval man may well have tried to express the subconscious intuition of thought or mind in his conception of Kami, for the mythology makes the Kami talk and act like human beings. In the primal stage of self-consciousness it would have been difficult to have made the initial start in developing the concept of mind as creator of the universe more adequately than by personifying the Kami. In many other mythologies, the Heavenly spirits or deities are made to talk; and though that has been one reason for modern skepticism's rejection of the truth in mythology, there is scientific justification now for revising this conclusion. If science is right in beginning to interpret the universe as "mind," primaeval man was obeying a sound instinct in picturing Heaven as an abode where conversation occurs, for we cannot think of mentality without thinking of a capacity to express ideas. Though the self-creative Heavenly mind in its pure subjectivity may not actually be vocal, nevertheless, primaeval Shinto gave the concept of mind to the creative impetus by depicting the Kami as talking in the Plain of High Heaven. Modern science cannot explain what it means by mind as creator except in the sense meant by Shinto in making use of the term Kami. The meaning in both cases is that the universe does not originate in materiality, but matter is an aspect of the immaterial creative spirit. Shinto, therefore, has as much right to use Kami as the source of the universe as science has to use mind or thought as it is now doing:

> The universe begins to look more like a great thought than like a great machine. Mind no longer appears as an accidental intruder into the realm of matter. We are beginning to suspect that we ought rather to hail it as the creator and governor of the realm of matter. . . . The old dualism of mind and matter . . . seems likely to disappear . . . through substantial matter resolving itself into a creation and manifestation of mind.[8]

Unlike science, Shinto never, in the past, has regarded the universe as a "great machine" and never has been dualistic. So Shinto does not have to change its conceptions in order to take the hand of science. It is science that is changing, and in doing so is becoming itself Shinto; for even though the vocabularies differ, there is no basic difference in the ideas that favour science at the expense of Shinto. In the light of the testimony modern science is offering, it is impossible to dismiss Shinto mythology as the outcome of ignorant, primitive imagination. Somehow, the subconscious knowledge that life has of itself was seeking expression; and the Shinto myth makers were following the right path, led by an inner intuition of reality. In one respect Shinto differs from the new scientific implication. The idea of mind as the "governor of the realm of matter" is

---

[8] Sir James Jeans, op .cit., pp. 158-9.

not Shinto, for Shinto sees the realm of matter as being itself Kami or in the scientific phrasing "mind." Here, science becomes confused, while Shinto holds steadily to the pure intuition. For matter cannot be a manifestation of mind and at the same time governed by mind, except in the sense of mind creating itself as matter and so governing or controlling itself. That is to say, there are not two aspects of mind, one as a manifestation of matter and another as the governor of matter, for if this were so, a form of dualism would result which modern science is seeking to deny. Shinto mythology, conceiving the entire universe as Kami has no need of the concept of a "governor" and therefore holds to pure monism. Shinto everywhere emphasizes the idea of self-creativeness of Kami and nowhere implies the existence of an omnipotent "governor":

> We have three distinct conceptions of creation in Japanese myths— first, as generation in the most literal sense; second, as reducing to order; and third, as growth.[9]

Humanity's experience confirms this process as the actual way of creative evolution. There is first, the self-creative appearance of life, as an initiating impetus. Then, as the result of effort, and by experience gained through struggle, there is organization. After organization takes place, growth becomes the final step in the creative progress of life. Human society advances in this way, and the Shinto myths describe the processes with considerable clearness. Initially, in the Shinto mythology, there is spontaneous creation and the originating impetus of growth appears. Thereafter, the myths personalize the process of reducing the world to order as a creative activity, not a mechanical process but a difficult task encountering many preliminary failures, for no omnipotent Heavenly guidance is tenable in Shinto. Conflict has to be overcome by conflict before orderly self-development or natural growth begins.

It is then that Shinto mythology describes the Divine Grandchild, Ninigi-no-Mikito, descending to earth. Doubtless in the story of Ninigi's descent from the Plain of High Heaven to Japan, the mythology mixes blurred racial memories of distant ancestors arriving in Japan from afar as a historical event, with pure intuition of humanity's origin. The primaeval mentality did not vision the ancestral evolution of mankind in any definitely discernible way. Yet, it is a curious fact that when Ninigi descended to earth, the welcome accorded him was by Saruta-Hiko-no-Kami, Monkey-Field Prince, who offered himself as Ninigi's vanguard.

---

[9] W. G. Aston, Shinto (in Religions Ancient and Modern Series), pp. 21-3.

Later, Saruta married Ame-no-Usume-no-Mikoto, famous Heavenly dancer, who accompanied Ninigi to earth and whose descendants bore the title of Saru, "Monkey." What the fundamental intuition behind this idea of associating monkey and man may have been it is impossible to say; but an evolutionary meaning is possible which the Shinto mythologists were unable to express with any accuracy. More important than any evolutionary idea, however, is the fact that in Ninigi, the Shinto mythology personalizes mankind as subjective, heavenly divine spirit emerging individualistically into the objective world and developing co-ordination through tribal and national growth.

Ninigi was accompanied to earth also by Omoi-kane-no-Kami, the Thought-Co-ordinator, who had previously given successful counsel at the first Kami assembly in Heaven when Amaterasu, the Heavenly Queen, hid herself in a cave and had to be enticed out. The Shinto tradition of divine democracy dates from this meeting. After exchanges of ideas, the Thought-Co-ordinator coordinated the suggestions of all the Kami and evolved the device of having Ame-no-Usume-no-Mikoto perform a comic dance in dishabille which caused all the Kami to roar with laughter, exciting Amaterasu's feminine curiosity, bringing her from the cave. The Thought-Co-ordinator is the Shinto personification of co-ordinated democratic rule as opposed to an absolutist domination of mankind. He was commissioned to take charge of government under Ninigi; and the Shinto conception of him as the divine creative spirit uniting the thoughts of all in a co-ordinated governing whole expresses the idea of democracy with accuracy and idealistic understanding. This part of the mythology clearly implies that the primaeval intuition sought to express the principle of divine creative spirit coming forth into earthly activities under the impulse of its own desire to progress in material ways by self-effort, without recourse to mechanical omnipotent power.

Other Kami had previously descended to earth, but they personify either divine spirit self-creating itself as matter, as Oho-yama-tsu-mi-no-Kami, the Great-Mountain-Possessor Kami, who is mountain itself, or else disorganized Kami, personifying individualism undergoing co-ordination. When co-ordination had acquired sufficient impetus and there was readiness for progressive growth, the mythology shows the third creative movement taking place in human relationships by the story of Ninigi. No idea of omnipotence is associated with him. Ninigi was not a Heavenly god sent to rule mankind. He personified mankind, as divine spirit starting from primitive conditions and depending not on omnipotent aid but on self-developed creative effort, experience and experiment for growth. The primitive architecture of Shinto Shrines symbolizes the same idea, as a perpetual reminder that though humanity began as divine spirit, yet the beginning was lowly, with freedom to choose between progress and inactivity.

The probability that the Ninigi myth contains some elements from primaeval history is increased by the mythological version that he married the daughter of the Great-Mountain-Possessor Kami—the personification of actual mountain. To describe a human being marrying the daughter of a mountain seems to suggest an absurd primitive lack of mentality; but the symbolism may contain fundamental truth. If the Ninigi myth makes use of a racial memory of overseas colonizers landing on the coast of Japan and settling in the country, then the conception of the new arrivals wedding themselves to the land is clearly expressed in the marriage of Ninigi to the daughter of the mountain. Even modern people often speak of being wedded to the rocks and dales of some homeland. To pioneers, crossing the sea in search of a new land for settlement, the sight of a mountain or rock is usually the first sign that a haven has been reached. The great respect paid by Shinto to rocks may well be the result of racial recollections of this kind.[10] Shinto shows profound understanding of spiritual depths of the human mind by making the settlement of courageous pioneer colonizers illustrate the spiritual beginning of organized life. In modern America, a significance not very different is symbolically given to Plymouth Rock, in Massachusetts, which marks the landing of the Pilgrims from the *Mayflower* in the Seventeenth Century. Plymouth Rock stirs deep spiritual emotions, as the symbol of commencement, of a new life of co-ordinated government, as does the Ninigi myth to those who understand Shinto.

This understanding is as much a part of Shinto today as it was in primal times. When modern democracy was being established as constitutional government in Japan in the Nineteenth Century, the great Emperor Meiji caused special emphasis to be placed on the divine beginning of government by establishing the *Genshi Sai* as the first festival of the year. *Genshi Sai* celebrates the descent of Ninigi to earth. The festival takes place in the Imperial Palace grounds at Tokyo, annually, on January third. This day was chosen because it immediately precedes the beginning of the official year of government, on January fourth, when

---

[10] This suggestion was made to the author by Dr. Ryusaku Tsunoda.

there is another annual ceremony, *Seiji-Hajime*, "Commencement of Affairs of State." That is to say, on the day before government begins, in Japan, formal respect is paid to divine creative spirit emerging from spaceless Heaven as humanity initiating national co-ordination whereby human progress attains its higher reaches.

Shinto constantly implies through its influence on the Japanese people that the progress of mankind is the intent of divine spirit on earth. Life is purposive to Shinto: a purposive activity of divine spirit seeking new expression in spirit's own self-created material world. Shinto does not believe human individuality is a mistake nor something to be magnified by losing itself in a mystical All. Nor does Shinto consider humanity's efforts to create new knowledge and to increase and satisfy new desires are the results of some mysterious divine error or evil influence. Shinto does not regard man as having been victimized by being born. Earthly life, to Shinto, is a desired satisfaction for divine spirit; and is a divine actuality in all of its manifestations, good and bad, whereby spirit creates its objective expansion by its own earthly efforts. Divine spirit, ever seeking renewal of creation, ever trying to progress in its material environment and ever striving to develop versatility of action—such is the emphasis Shinto gives to life.

Because Shinto embodies this subconsciously understood creative principle, it is able to retain its primaeval intuitive power in the modern era of Japan's national development. The modern mind, thanks to the researches of Bergson, is bringing to the light of self-consciousness an understanding of creative action which is in harmony with the subconscious impetus of Shinto. To know the modern philosophy of creative action in its spiritual sense is to understand the primaeval intuition of life that Shinto mythology struggled to express:

> Life is creation; life is hunger for creation; it cannot be maintained save by continually renewing and going beyond its present self, in accordance with the initial impulse it has received. . . . We experience this creative power within ourselves whenever we execute a free act. . . . Creation is not relegated to a mythical past. It prolongs itself around us, in us, in a welling forth of unforeseeable innovations, in the very power that prevents our habits, our acts, heredity, matter from fettering us, and transforms these obstacles into stimuli.[11]

---

[11] Jacques Chevalier, Henri Bergson, translated by Lilian A. Clare, pp. 264-5.

Shinto implies this same knowledge of life, not self-consciously expressed in such adequate words, but in its subconscious influence on self-development and creative action. Ever in Shinto the impulse of self to go beyond its present self is revealed in the mythology and by the history of the Japanese people who have responded to the Shinto creative impetus within themselves throughout their national existence. Shinto never has given expression to its creative principle in any formal philosophy. It seeks direct results in practical ways. The primaeval knowledge manifests itself through subconscious intuition which inspires creative action; and in various symbolic forms peculiar to itself, Shinto shows how clear is the understanding.

Thus, at Ise, where the most revered of the Shinto Shrines to Amaterasu-o-mi-Kami is situated, there is also a shrine, very close to the Amaterasu structure, dedicated to Ara-Mitama, the "Rough Divine Spirit," representing the active or progressive side of Shinto—the impetus of creative action. Its importance is shown by the respect paid to it; for when Imperial offerings are made at the Amaterasu-o-mi-Kami Shrine, similar offerings are made to Ara-Mitama. The fact that Shinto thus specially honours the Rough Divine Spirit shows how fundamentally right is the Shinto conception of the way creative action develops material progress. For expansion of creative activity is always along rough pathways where hardihood and endurance are essential to gain success. Painful effort must be put forth to overcome the difficulties blocking the road of progress; and the rough side of personality must be invoked to advance the cause of human welfare against the resistances of passivity and reaction. By personalizing creative action in this manner through respect paid to the Rough Divine Spirit, Shinto makes the Shrine a perpetual reminder of its right understanding of life and human nature.

Yet, in Shinto, the Nigi-Mitama, the "Gentle Divine Spirit" always accompanies the Rough Divine Spirit in the same individual; for without the former to balance the latter, humanity would be overwhelmed by roughness, making progress wholly materialistic. Nevertheless, more persistent effort is necessary to develop the Rough Divine Spirit and far greater energy must be acquired for the purposes of creative action than for gentility. Shinto expresses this fact by associating the Ara-Mitama Shrine with Amaterasu-o-mi-Kami at Ise—for Amaterasu is the Sun Kami and it is from the sun that life on earth secures the necessary energy to develop creative action. Creative action and the source of life's energy, personalized in association at the most venerated Shinto centre in Japan, are not the consequence of chance, but are responses to the primaeval subconscious knowledge that life has of creative action. The Rough Divine Spirit concept is very old in Shinto. The Ara-Mitama Shrine at Ise is of ancient design in pure Shinto style, and Shinto mythology shows the idea had become fixed in legend at an early date. When the Empress Jingo made her legendary conquest of Korea in the Third Century, A.D., the mythology says she established the Ara-Mitama of three Kami, before her departure, as the guardians the country.[12] The implication is that she tried to inspire in the people the Japanese spirit of effort to preserve order and stimulate action. Whether the legend of the Empress Jingo's invasion be true or false, the story testifies to the early Japanese conception of the Rough Divine Spirit as the impetus of action. Later, Korea sent cultural influences to Japan that may be described as the fruits of the Gentle Divine Spirit in Korea, which Japan accepted. Korea, however, was not competent to learn in exchange from Japan the invaluable advantage of stimulating the Rough Divine Spirit; and it is only within the present century that Japan has been able to instruct the Koreans in ways of creative activity.

Because all men are Kami or divine spirit does not mean to Shinto that all have equal powers as Rough Divine Spirit and Gentle Divine Spirit. Divinity means equality in the fact that all mankind is divine spirit of Heavenly origin. But, freedom of development which the creative impetus requires, and differences of environment and training, as well as physical disparities and the complexities of inherited traits all lead to inequalities. Divinity does not mean perfection in Shinto. There is no preordained way of Heavenly success on earth, for that would make divine spirit a machine, controlled by Fate or omnipotence. Self-consciousness has difficulty accepting this principle, for the tendency of self-conscious speculation is to make man into a dualistic individual, partly material and partly spiritual, and to conclude that the material part is imperfect while the spiritual part must be perfect. Shinto does not accept any such doctrine. The pure subconscious intuition of Shinto implies that divine spirit cannot be two different entities—material and spiritual. Divine spirit in material form is always divine spirit and nothing else. It is the subjective spirit of Heaven come forth into objectivity, starting with no preordained powers, but self-creating its own ideas of progress and its own instruments for advancement, and able to

---

[12] Kojiki, 2nd edition, B. H. Chamberlain's translation, pp. 282-3.

fail as well as succeed without, in any sense, losing its divinity.

The subconscious knowledge life has of itself has been gained by racial experience and by direct subjective contact with life's origin and with materiality. This does not mean there is subconscious knowledge of the future, except in cases where the future is mechanistic or stabilized, and is controlled by past or present events, as sometimes happens. But, no omnipotent competence to foresee the future as the path of life still to be created exists in subconscious intuition, according to Shinto. Life never knows its own future, when the creative impetus is inspiring man to fresh effort. Otherwise there would not be so many discarded experiments scattered along the evolutionary pathway of progress. To try to pry into the subconscious mind or into Heaven for secret means of knowing the future so that self-consciousness can unlock the doors of Fate is a vain effort. There is no certain knowledge of the future in the creative present. The search is a device of the self-conscious mind seeking to save itself the pains and difficulties of learning by experience; but life never has gained the benefits of progress automatically. Individuals, here and there, may gamble and win occasionally. But, for life itself, there are no doors of Fate to unlock unless life is content to mechanize itself and abandon its freedom.

Shinto never has implied that divine spirit knows the future. When the Heavenly Grandchild, Ninigi, was about to depart from Heaven to earth, Heavenly knowledge was insufficient to determine the cause of a nearby disturbance which the mythology describes as delaying his start. An inquiry had to be made, and instead of discovering any opposition to Ninigi, it was found that a welcome was being prepared. Since the Heavenly Kami were unable to know what was happening advantageously in the present, so near at hand, how can Heaven know the distant future in Shinto? The subconscious mind cannot discern what self-consciousness will create in advance for there is always an element of spontaneity, of something absolutely new in the creative process. This, indeed, is what the word creative means. If Shinto were to turn from this conception it would be destroyed by mechanism. Divination rites and the use of charms are always present in primitive cultures and they found their way into early Japanese culture, but they were due to lack of complete understanding of the Shinto intuition.

There is some reason to believe that the comic dance of Ame-no-Usume-no-Mikoto before the cave of Amaterasu was really intended as a ridiculing parody of "divine possession"; and it was probably this element in it that caused such hilarity among the Heavenly Kami.[13] Since Shinto conceives all life to be divine spirit, it is impossible for divine spirit to enter into certain individuals to take command of their minds, for they always have been divine spirit. Yet, primitive belief in magic has been encouraged in Japan especially because of Chinese influences. In China, however, there has been no counteracting stimulant such as the Shinto creative impetus provided in Japan. So, China has felt the full effect of this devastating debasement while Japan has always struggled against it. Nevertheless, Shinto's loyalty to subconsciousness has acted to restrain Shinto from interfering as much as it might with self-conscious demands for magic. What little self-conscious expressiveness Shinto has shown has retained very largely the primitive influence. The real power of Shinto has always lodged in the subconscious knowledge life has of itself, but this has not prevented occasional surface manifestations that seemingly have run counter to the direct intuition of creative action. Yet, we know so little about the human mind's ways of stimulating itself that the very persistence of human nature in calling for charms and incantations may have been due to an important use the mind had for them in primitive times. This tendency still continues even in advanced utilitarian civilizations:

> In New York City, the Catholics have invaded the motor-minded pub-
> lic, and on .February 8, 1931, the Church of the Holy Family, on East
> 47th Street, began a series of monthly motor-services by blessing sixty
> parked cars. Holy water was cast in the direction of the automobiles,
> while the priest uttered the following prayer: "O God, our Lord, vouch-
> safe to hear our prayer and bless this vehicle with Thy right hand and
> bid Thy angels stand by to save and protect from danger all those who
> travel in it." [14]

Self-confidence is a mysterious element in human life. Some mentalities seem naturally to possess it; others acquire it in many ways, not the least important being through belief in themselves inspired by external sources. Even in sophisticated, highly educated circles where charms and invocations are regarded as superstitions, the physician trained in psychology who has developed a "bed-side manner," may greatly assist

---

[13]   B. H. Chamberlain says of this dance that "the imitation and not the reality of divine possession appears to be here intended." Kojiki, 2nd edition, Chamberlain's translation, p. 69, note 32.

[14]   Jay Franklin, "Catholic or Protestant," The Forum Magazine (New York), September, 1931.

cures by the suggestiveness of his behaviour. Civilized man is akin to the primitive in many mental responses whose basic meanings are unknown:

> Nearly as much as the primitive, he (civilized man) is beset by disturbing contents and therefore needs just as many apotropaic charms. He no longer works the magic with medicine bags, amulets and animal sacrifices, but with nerve-remedies, neuroses, "enlightenment" cults of the will, etc.[15]

As successful creative action engenders increasing self-conscious efficiency, life gradually severs itself from such stimulants and the mind becomes more self-reliant. Until that fortunate time is reached, however, humanity will continue to respond to the primitive inheritance of ways to cajole the mind into becoming self-confident. To discourage the use of charms and to leach the people to trust themselves, however, is to follow the progressive spirit of Shinto.

Yet, since every way of life is a way of divine spirit, there can be no activity that is not Shinto, however crude, however mistaken or however noble and potent it may be. Shinto, however, as the way of divine spirit at the cross-road of life, has two aspects, the subconscious and the self-conscious. These two must be separately identified in order to understand that one way of life is called Shinto and another way "not Shinto." Mankind's creative impetus and the knowledge life has of subjective reality are subconscious and intuitive. But, the expansion of versatile activity and self-development that life seeks are objective. Some degree of self-consciousness is necessary to life's progress. The activities of mankind are not controlled by subconscious power within but are inspired principally by conscious desires and by attractions or disillusionments of the objective world. In struggling to advance, man is following the impetus of action within subconsciousness; but the conscious mind can reject the subconscious influence and can imagine its own principles of life any way it wishes. In this sense, there is rivalry between the subconscious intuition and the conscious surface of the mind. Too, the conscious mind, because of its experiences with objective reality, has its own problems to solve and frequently has not acquired sufficient knowledge to understand how the subconscious intuition of subjective reality can be interpreted to solve the surface difficulties dealing with spirituality and ethics and human relationships in general. So, conflicts arise on the mind's

---

[15] C. G. Jung, op. cit., p. 123.

surface and self-consciousness may turn from the primaeval subconscious intuition of creative action and the spiritual divinity of all existence. Beneath the surface, within the subconscious depths of the mind, life has direct immediacy of knowledge of itself, as divine spirit come forth from subjectivity and materializing itself for objective action. Subconsciousness seeks to impart its knowledge to self-consciousness, as a stimulus for activity and to permit the self-conscious mind to gain inspiration by realizing its true being. When the primaeval subconscious intuition exerts its influence on man, either self-consciously or in terms of unanalysed responses, then the results are Shinto. But when self-consciousness goes its own way, heedless of the intuition of subjective reality, then the consequences must be called "not Shinto," in the sense that they are not reconcilable with life's inner knowledge of itself.

Yet, the expression "not Shinto" is correct only when it has the limited meaning that self-consciousness has not come into full contact with the subconscious truth. Fundamentally, every action of life is Shinto, in that it is a choice at the cross-road, exercised by divine spirit. Every denial of Shinto is at the same time Shinto; for the denial is no more than a way of divine spirit experimenting on the surface of life to find explanations of existence that temporarily may satisfy some demand of self-consciousness. We say an individual who performs some reprehensible act is "not human," while at the same time he is human and always must be human. So it is with Shinto. Every activity whether advantageous or reprehensible is a way of divine spirit on earth; but some activities show such deviations from subconscious knowledge that they may be called "not Shinto." Nevertheless, the purpose in using the term "not Shinto" is only to recall self-consciousness into a closer association with the subconscious truth, for the two must be coordinated if life is to attain its higher levels of self-development.

Self-consciousness cannot be forced against its will to accept the truth that primaeval subconscious intuition endeavours to send to the mind's surface, if real self-development is to result. Self-consciousness must be convinced in accordance with its objective understanding of existence. Shinto, however, has not taken the initiative in seeking to convince modern self-consciousness, because the Japanese have been contented with the subconscious intuition and have not developed self-consciousness within their own culture to any expansive analytical extent. So, realization of the fundamental implications of Shinto, in terms acceptable to modern comprehension has never existed. Indeed, only in the present

age of self-conscious understanding of creative action and by the aid of
the new conceptions of science has it been possible to acquire self-conscious understanding of the Shinto intuition that the primaeval
subconscious mind endeavoured to express in mythological form. Self-
consciousness, however, can now proceed, with existing knowledge, to
clarify Shinto, and add to humanity's realization of the living truth of
spiritual reality as the subconscious intuition revealed it to our primaeval ancestors when the human mind was attuned to life's innate
comprehension of itself.

CHAPTER IV

SHINTO AND RELIGION

SHINTO shows no evidence of having originated as an analytical effort of self-consciousness to fix man's place in the universe or to provide a haven for the human soul in distress. Shinto does not philosophize nor moralize about life nor does it attempt to establish a relationship between man and divinity as a deliberate purpose. Primaeval man did not resolve to discover his own spirit or the divine or to find meanings in existence in formulating the Shinto mythology. His intent was to put into permanent form confused recollections of historical occurrences and to trace the ancestry and development of the Japanese race and explain how Japan itself came into being. The initiative in formulating a spiritual conception to give expression to this purpose cannot have come from a self-conscious resolve to make spirituality the basis of the narrative, for primaeval man had no such mental capacity. Rather, it seems that the direct knowledge life has of itself and of subjective reality rose as an immediacy of intuition to inspire the spiritual character of the Shinto mythology. Primaeval man accepted what came forth from the subconscious depths without showing any critical ability and formulated it as best he could with no logical self-conscious aid.

Shinto, therefore, is not a spiritual guide book prepared to satisfy self-conscious yearnings to overcome the contradictions of earthly existence. Yet, Shinto is wholly spiritual in its subconscious realization that the entire universe is divine spirit. Since it has remained a subconscious power, moulding Japanese culture from within as a silent, invisible impetus, Shinto has not generally supplied the needs of the human mind for self-conscious spiritual explanations of the universe and man's position in life and after death. Shinto has not simplified or analysed its intuitive truths, whose meanings have seldom been understood by self-consciousness.

As man overcomes the primaeval limitations of inexpressive mentality, however, and develops wider outlooks, he begins to ask questions about existence and the reasons for humanity's hardships and the mysterious ways of Nature. Relations among men become complex and inimical. Rough individualism causes man to inflict cruelties on man.

The mind and the body suffer during the painful struggles for progress. Those in authority oppress the weak and ignorant; and the rich frequently gain their wealth by crushing the defenseless. Life is an endless state of misery for vast numbers of people. These conditions result because life is not mechanistic but must make its way by experience and experiment, while individualism and co-ordination struggle for their own separate rights. Life thus progresses at its own expense, penalizing itself for its own inefficiencies as a spur to creative action.

Often, the hardships of progress deter man from continuing to advance; but when the creative impetus is suppressed, in this way, demoralization, debasements and decay destroy the nations and races that turn to mechanism. To hold loyally to the cause of creative action despite the inflictions it imposes, man must devise ways of sustaining his self-confidence and maintaining his moral courage. Shinto, however, offered no adequate aid to the afflicted during the early evolution of culture in Japan. Being predominantly subconscious in its understanding of life, Shinto did not expand its meanings to meet self-conscious demands for mental support amid the complexities of progress. The unhappiness and confusions that mankind encounters would not exist if self-consciousness were in abeyance. Though the Japanese have not developed the intensity of self-consciousness that prevails in the West nor the liking for analysis, nevertheless sufficient self-conscious pressure has persisted in Japan to cause the people to desire more detailed surface explanations of existence than the subconscious intuition of Shinto has been able to elevate from its subjective depths.

Under this condition, people turn to religions. Religious development is the outcome of effort by the self-conscious mind to fix man's place in the universe in satisfying terms when the mind is troubled by objective uncertainties and seeks explanations of existence consistent with the self-conscious knowledge of the times. The subconscious intuition that man is more than materiality keeps rising to the mind's surface, but man wants self-consciously more than this single fact. He enquires of himself how this subconscious knowledge fits in with common experiences of the triumphs and disappointments and tragedies of life. He seeks meanings which subconsciousness does not supply; for the more self-consciousness develops, the more it tends to move further and further from the subconscious—and the subconscious ways of communicating the knowledge that life has of itself are always difficult for self-consciousness to understand.

In times of trouble and grave perplexity, mankind seeks leaders to find solutions of the unsolved problems of life. This is especially so when spiritual issues are involved. Spirituality concerns the difficulties of reconciling subjective feelings and objective actions, the most bewildering enigma of man's moral life. So, reformers, prophets and creators of new spiritual conceptions arise; and when they express principles that console the suffering and satisfy longings for future rewards to compensate for earthly miseries, they are regarded as being inspired and may even be deified. Their followers seek to establish the solacing teachings beyond controversy by self-conscious doubters, and summon faith to their aid, for faith has the inestimable advantage of keeping the mind self-confident when it has no answer for disturbing criticism. Makers of religions are the products of their different eras and environments, but they usually associate two common elements with their doctrines. They comfort the oppressed and give assurances of satisfactions after death for those who live in accordance with the commands of their creeds. Some religions, too, have inspired their followers to the noblest ways of living by moral precepts and have provided art and civilization with an impetus of cultural development of the most valuable kind.

Religions, indeed, have given to self-consciousness a soul. They came into being when self-consciousness was evolving amid confused surroundings; and man reaching out into the newly discovered universe of creative action, became afraid—not of the universe but of the difficulties of human progress. Religions evolved out of the demand of self-consciousness for support amid the tribulations of creative action and the pressure of the subconscious creative impetus for self-development. At times, religions have found it too difficult to stimulate man to undergo the painful effort of increasing his material desires, and so they have tried to overcome suffering by doctrines based on suppression of desires. Creative action has suffered by this backward swing of religious teachings. Nevertheless, the aim of religion always has been to lighten humanity's earthly burdens by causing self-consciousness to realize that man is more than matter; and so, through religion, self-consciousness has come to know some spiritual values and to interest itself in the soul of mankind.

Yet, so dominating is the creative impetus that it seizes upon religion itself as an instrument for selfish action. Under this impulse, religions have become organized movements and the followers frequently have engaged in rivalries and conflicts similar to those that mark the struggles of life in secular fields. Efforts are made to dominate others by weight of authority and by imposing creeds upon mankind much as autocratic rulers inflict their arbitrary wills on their subjects. It has often happened that abominable mental and physical cruelties have been practised by religious enthusiasts on those who have sought to maintain their own freedom of thought and action. The great creators of religions have moved into life's subconscious depths, seeking truth; but when the truth reaches the surface it usually passes into the control of expositors and commentators who reshape it to accord with their own ideas and reinterpret it in ways that seek to become authoritative. For mankind frequently wants to be guided by authority rather than by truth. Religious authority releases man from the painful difficulty of enquiring into meanings. Spiritual truth requires individual responsibility for its acceptance. Religions almost invariably teach that man is both material and spiritual and that the material bodies or material desires must be subordinated to the spiritual. So, in this respect, man and the divine are separated by religions, despite the instinct in all religions for unification of humanity and spirituality. Self-consciousness always endeavours to separate in order to act, and the self-conscious mind thus tends to divide spaceless spirit from spatial matter, seeking to comprehend spirit as a distinctive entity in itself. Great spiritual leaders try to overcome this separatist tendency but such efforts are very hard for self-consciousness to understand.

Yet, as mankind's activities become more efficient and as education spreads, the path of spiritual progress becomes less difficult. The mind grows more self-confident and the power of authority in religion declines. Mankind turns within himself for spiritual comfort and seeks to know himself by inner communion. There is need for priestly help in this search of the individual to recognize spiritual truth by his own understanding, for the broad-minded priest knows that there is no monopoly of spirituality in any fixed, inflexible creed. Somewhat as the modern physician helps Nature to cure the patient, so the modern priest responds to the new spiritual needs of progress by instructing the people how to undertake the responsibility of curing themselves, spiritually:

The foundation of everything lies in elucidating our own soul.[1]

The advantages organized religions have bestowed on mankind have often been of decisive value in times of past crises of the human spirit

---

[1] Rev. Haya Akegarasu, *Man Above Gods*, Lectures at Zintei School, Okayama, Japan, 1925.

and still may be in the future. But for the trained priesthood, devising spiritual comfort for humanity's dire need, it is doubtful whether mankind could have endured the pains of self-development against autocracy and despotism. Man's faith in humanity as a vital force amid the early struggles of self-consciousness to understand existence has been largely due to religion.

Shinto, however, has not sought to serve self-conscious needs in any such organized way. Its influence as a subconscious intuition would have been endangered had it been subjected to doctrinal devices to adjust it to surface demands of the mind. Shinto has exerted important influences subconsciously on Japanese responses to religious and ethical ideas imported from without, but it has not competed with them self-consciously. During the early period of Japan's development, when the people were isolated culturally from the continent, the subconscious power of Shinto was insufficient to cause ethical reactions to the sufferings of life. The Shinto emphasis on purification and Shinto's predominant interest in living reality were not self-consciously understood; and the consequence was a misinterpretation of the idea of defilement;

> The revulsion of feeling awakened at the sight of persons afflicted with contagious diseases, the issue of blood at child birth, the commission of grave crimes, or the presence of a dead body, came to be associated with notions of impurity, which, while demanding rigorous riles for purification, tended to a hardening of the heart toward the victims of life's misfortunes, which often meant heartless cruelty. A Rescript issued by the Emperor Kotoku in 646, after enumerating various evils such as the foregoing being due to mistaken notions about purification, especially forbids them. The tenderer sympathies of men, thus turned into arid wastes, were congenial soil for Buddhism when it came in with its gospel of compassion for all men in all the vicissitudes life, and its gospel of hope for men beyond the tomb.[2]

The ethical inertia of the time was not due to any moral defect in the Japanese temperament, for otherwise Buddhism and Confucianism would not have been so enthusiastically received. The responsibility rested on the lack of self-conscious analytical power to give expression to the inner implications of Shinto. Since all men are divine spirit, helpfulness to overcome the defects of inexperience and the errors of ignorance, is a natural corollary of Shinto; but no doctrine of this kind had been

---

[2] Rev. Harper H. Coates and Rev. Ryugaku Ishizuka, *Honen, the Buddhist Saint,* 2nd edition, p. 9.

developed in Japan because Shinto remained subconsciously inarticulate to explain its meanings. Buddhism and Confucianism had undergone self-conscious development for more than a thousand years when they entered Japan and thus had highly developed codes of spiritual and ethical principles for self-consciousness to understand, in keeping with the knowledge of the era.

Yet, without the subconscious intuition of Shinto holding Japan steadily loyal to creative action and the tradition of the nation's divine ancestry, Buddhism and Confucianism could not have been adequately reinterpreted in ways to sustain progress, and continental degeneration might have settled in the islands. Shinto's very lack of self-conscious expression had kept the Japanese surface mind free to reformulate the foreign doctrines. Too, the primaeval mental simplicity of the Japanese, and the direct knowledge of life lodged in Shinto, caused Japan to discern in Buddhism and Confucianism fundamental meanings that had become atrophied on the continent because of over-sophistication. The re-interpretations of the doctrines gave peace to the surface mind, because Shinto has no creed, no formal ethical doctrine, no theology of any kind. It has certain forms of observances, but they are not ecclesiastical, for there are no deities in Shinto: man and divine spirit are the same. The observances are based on the subconscious truth that the entire universe is divine spirit and that living, earthly spirit should pay respect to the continuity of spirit as a self-developing process from the Heavenly beginnings to the present time.

At times, people have engaged in ecclesiastical devotions at Shinto Shrines on their own initiative; but this has always been an individual attitude and is a misinterpretation of the Shinto meaning. When it is understood that man and the divine are the same, there can be no worship, though there can be modes of showing respect and concentrating the self-conscious mind on its spiritual being and its divine ancestry. Were deities to be forced on Shinto, the fundamental significance of the primaeval conception that the universe is Kami or divine spirit would have to be changed. The result would be a dualistic idea, based on an artificial dogma destroying the Shinto principle that mankind is Kami or divine spirit in the material world. In its subconscious power, Shinto, however, never has deviated far from the intuitive knowledge that man and the divine are not two. Man always is divine spirit on earth; not the ecclesiastical divine spirit which is regarded as omnipotent and always changeless in its purity, but divine spirit self-developing and making its own way by creative action. Divine spirit on earth keeps itself pure only by constant effort. It creates its own purity and can become impure through lack of experience and by engaging in experimental processes in search of progress that leads to temporary defilements. Shinto thus indicates that it understands the direct intuitive truth that purity is not a mechanical process automatically preserving divine spirit in a state of machine-like innocence. Purification must be earned; it is an ever-present ideal to keep the self-conscious mind from lingering in debasements. So, the frequent purification ceremonies in Shinto have the meaning that divine spirit on earth, while struggling to make progress must ever remind its self-conscious self that impurities retard spirit's earthly self-development. Sometimes, formalism has entered into the purification conception of Shinto and then the basic meaning is partly lost; but under no circumstance can the idea of worship be associated with purification rites while the fundamental idea of Shinto remains that man and Kami or divine spirit are the same.

The Shinto conception that Kami or divine spirit can be impure seems strange to inherited ecclesiastical tradition which holds man to be in part a material being dwelling away from ever immaculate and perfect divinity. It may appear to suggest that Shinto is lacking in true spirituality, whereas Shinto is wholly spiritual in its understanding. If divine spirit be the entire universe, then whatever is impure is divine just as much as whatever is pure. There is no other possible meaning of life if the universe be monistic and if humanity be spiritual in origin. Divine spirit, as self-creative, must make its own way, and when the way is not mechanical and therefore not known in advance, mistakes and errors are the consequence. If divine spirit be free, and if it seeks progress, risks must be taken, for progress is the outcome of a process of trial and error. The mind is affected by these failures and tends to consider they mean man has a dual nature, materialistic, which is the cause of impurities, and spiritual, which ever tries to purify humanity. This is not the primaeval intuition expressed in Shinto. Man, according to Shinto, is divine spirit or Kami on earth; and the impurities that soil the self-conscious mind and the objective activities of divine spirit are the outcome of spirit's inexperience and lack of self-creative knowledge in the new environments that divine spirit itself generates in its experimental attempts to expand progress and self-development. They are the waste that life ever is trying to throw away. The Shinto purification ceremony assists the mind in getting rid of this waste, but the procedure does not mean that divine spirit worships divine spirit by purifying its self-conscious mind:

> Worship (in Shinto) applies both to the forms of courtesy and respect
> towards human beings and of reverence for the gods (Kami). Indeed,
> the latter is not a separate kind of worship, but is composed almost
> exclusively of the same elements in a new application. Nearly every-
> thing in the worship of the gods (Kami) is borrowed from the forms of
> social respect. . . . The simplest and most universal mode of showing
> reverence to the gods (Kami) is by bowing.[3]

There could be no clearer indication of the Shinto conception that
man and divine spirit are the same. No adoration of aloof deities takes
place when reverence is paid to Heavenly divine spirit. Divine spirit
respects its own divinity by means shown in social relations, except that
when the object of respect is Heavenly divinity, there is a special mental
impression of spiritual idealism which emphasizes to the self-conscious
mind the responsibilities of divine spirit on earth for carrying forward
spirit's objective self-development. We display reverence for the living
who inspire us and for whom we have affection. So in Shinto reverence
is manifested for Heavenly divine spirit and for the continuity of divine
spirit on earth. The late Marquis Okuma, explaining the attitude to be
observed at Shinto Shrines, declared it should not be religious worship
in the ordinary sense but *Keishin,* "reverence":

> To attempt by means of prayers to drive away sickness or to pray for
> prosperity and happiness is mere superstition and is a violation of the
> nature of reverence. Reverence is not a kind of religious faith.[4]

Clapping hands before a Shinto Shrine often is misinterpreted as meaning the devotee wishes to call the attention of the Shrine divine spirit to
himself; but W. G. Aston has shown that clapping hands is an ancient,
form of paying respect in Japan;[5] and it is associated, as well, in the
modern world with sudden joy not only among children but also among
adults. Food and other offerings at Shinto Shrines are not intended for
the physical gratification of spaceless spirit. They should be interpreted
as marks of respect before the mystery of life generating and sustaining
itself. To regard them as being intended for the enjoyment of Heavenly
divine spirit is a superstition:

---

[3] W. G. Aston, *Shinto: They Way of the Gods,* pp. 208-9.

[4] Quoted by Rev. D. C. Holtom, D.D., in "The Political Philosphy of Modern Shinto,"
Transactions of the Asiatic Society of Japan, Vol. XLIX, Part II, pp. 86-7.

[5] *Shinto: The Way of the Gods,* p. 209.

Offerings were in the older Shinto regarded as tokens of respect and were not supposed to be eaten, worn or otherwise enjoyed by the deity.[6]

There are no prayers in a religious sense in Shinto, for prayers are petitions from humanity to a separated deity. Shinto does not separate humanity from divinity and ecclesiastical praying is therefore impossible in pure Shinto. Shinto priests recite *norito,* which are forms of paying respect and expressing gratitude for divine spirit's assistance to divine spirit, somewhat as we return thanks for man's help to man. For, to Shinto, all life is a continuity of action, and we should be grateful to divine spirit of the past whose activities have been helpful to us in the present. The food we eat is divine spirit sustaining divine spirit and we, the centres of divine spirit who benefit, ought to express thanks for this assistance. But, *norito* are not petitions from humanity asking Heavenly favours for the devout, nor pleas for salvation, nor requests for Heavenly mercy, nor for rewards after death.

Shinto is preparation for life; religions are preparation for death. In Japan, weddings are usually celebrated according to Shinto rites and babies are taken to Shinto Shrines, since weddings and births are life renewing itself. Funerals are almost always conducted in accordance with Buddhist or Christian ceremonies. There are no cemeteries at Shinto Shrines. When Shinto funerals are held, the body is elevated to the height of the Kami symbol of divine spirit in the Shrine, indicating that there is no difference between the human spirit and the divine.

Shinto recoils from death. To orthodox theology, life has an element of materialistic pollution separating it from divine spirit, while death has a sacred significance as the departure of the soul from earthly temptations to the realm of spiritual purity. Shinto reverses this attitude. Shinto sees death as pollution and regards life as the realm where divine spirit seeks to purify itself by rightful self-development. Shinto wants individual human life to be prolonged forever on earth as a victory of divine spirit in preserving its objective personality in its highest forms. Divine spirit has not yet discovered how to create eternal life on earth for itself in personal embodiments, but:

As improvements that may reasonably be anticipated if man is willing to aim at them, we may enumerate . . . the practical conquest of all diseases and in consequence a great extension of human life. A conquest of death it might be rash to promise, although it has already come to

---

[6] W. G. Aston, *Shinto* (in Religions Ancient and Modern Series), p. 59.

seem a mystery why anyone should die. Why should the individual die when the race is deathless? Is not he also a self-repairing machine— and once he has learnt that magic art of which *our* machines remain incapable, why should not his body continue to repair itself forever, and even grow more expert in so doing? Why should it relax its efforts to keep alive after a while, and allow itself to get clogged up more and more with the waste products of its own working until it ceases to function and dies a "natural" death?[7]

Were divine spirit on earth to conquer death, all religions would be compelled to change their conceptions of spirit, but not Shinto. When the creative impetus discovers how to prolong human life indefinitely, the Shinto conception of death as pollution will be understood in its true meaning. For, as Shinto understands human life to be the culminating attainment of divine spirit's objective expansion, so death is the gravest threat to its progressive development. Shinto senses the time when death will be conquered on earth, accelerating progress by permitting indefi- nite personal self-development and abolishing the waste of effort now concentrated in over-population as a guarantee of racial survival.

The most vivid story in Shinto mythology narrates the first appear- ance of death, when Izanami—the Shinto Eve—died while giving birth to the Kami of fire and disappeared in the land of Yomi. The myth relates how her husband Izanagi searched for her and pleaded for her to return. Izanami agreed to try to do so if Izanagi would not look at her corpse. Impatient at her long delay, however, Izanagi looked and, appalled at the sight, fled, pursued by the spirits of Yomi and by Izanami, barely escap- ing from their vindictive fury. The myth shows evidence of representing a dream. Millions of husbands have followed their deceased wives simi- larly to the land of Yomi, for the orthodox Japanese derivation of Yomi is from *Yoru,* "night."[8] That is to say, while asleep, bereaved husbands have been carried in their dreams to the graves of their wives. Pleading with the wife to return to life, the husband has secured her promise in the dream, but the promise not materializing, he has uncovered the grave and terrorized by the sight, has fled pursued by the imaginary dream spirits of the dead. There is nothing unusual in such an incident; and it is characteristic of the Shinto desire to hold fast to life as the objective sphere of divine spirit, that the pollution of death should be emphasized

[7] F. C. S. Schiller, "Man's Future on Earth," *The Personalist Magazine,* April, 1933, pp. 125-6.

[8] B. H Chamberlain, *Kojiki,* 2nd edition, p. 40, note 1.

so like a dream as to make the experience of the defilement of death a common one. That a dream basis may be involved is further suggested by the mythological account of Izanagi alone giving birth to children after his vain effort to recover his wife. Yet, in Shinto, there is no spiritual extinction in death. The body's decay is the mark of divine spirit's failure to hold itself in personalized material form for earthly activities and is also a clearing of the ground for life's renewed experiments in progressive evolution when the body no longer can retain sufficient vitality for creative action. But Shinto does not indicate that divine spirit ceases to exist after earthly effort terminates, for the "Land of Yomi," where death abides, is not a place of annihilation, since Izanagi found Izanami there. Shinto, however, does not speculate about happenings after the individual's life on earth ends, for Shinto's dominating interest is in divine spirit's objective self-development in the living universe. Shinto wants life to live, not to die. This attitude is hard for self-consciousness to understand ecclesiastically. Mankind knows the inevitability of life's passing and longs for spiritual comfort when earthly ties are severed. Religions, therefore, play important parts in devising spiritual terms that soothe grief in bereavements and keep humanity gentle-hearted with facing death, for those who require to be tranquillized. But, Shinto does not concern itself with softening the sting of death. Shinto leaves to self-consciousness the problem of consoling itself and concentrates its attention on strengthening the subconscious intuition that divine spirit seeks for itself living activity.

Respect paid to trees by Shinto is a continuous reminder, dating from primal times, of the Shinto emphasis on life, and is acknowledgment as well that not only man but Nature also is divine spirit. Trees that surround Shinto Shrines in verdant groves, are not deified nor is any form of "Nature worship" associated with the esteem shown for them. To call the trees "sacred" is not to sanctify them, but emphasizes the Shinto conception that the entire universe is the living spirit of divinity. As Shinto sees the success of divine spirit in its material manifestations in terms of life's power to develop itself on earth, so the strength and vigour of noble trees make them appropriate symbols to surround Shinto Shrines where they are always found in towering majesty.

> In general it may be said that a tree is regarded as sacred in proportion
> as it manifests life. Evidence of extraordinary vital powers may appear
> to the prescientific mind in such features as great age, abnormal size,
> special hardihood, as for example the retention of verdure throughout

the seasons by the evergreens, or finally in some strange shape or promi-
nent characteristic which induces in the beholder an unusual attitude
of awareness. . . . The distinctive sacred tree of Shinto is known to the
Japanese language as *sakaki*. . . . The quality of sacredness as originally attributed to the *sakaki* is undoubtedly due to the fact that it is an
evergreen. . . . *Saka* is evidently the root of the verb *sakaeru*, "to flour-
ish," "to lie full of life"; *ki* is, of course, "tree." . . . Though the old
order passes, giving place to the new, yet we must admit that after all,
to most of us there is something worshipful about a tree. The largest
and most ancient manifestations of life that come within range of our
observation on earth today are trees. Where find a better symbol of
renewing, resurgent, enduring life than a tree? The old "tree of life"
may become for modern man at least a symbol of life.[9]

Upright and steadfast, blossoming in adversity and nourishing as the
tempest rages, providing from its abundance for those who safeguard its
thriving life, the Shinto tree is a perpetual reminder to mankind of right
conduct. When one pays respect to a Shinto Shrine, a branch of the sakaki
tree is placed on a small table before the Shrine, the end of the stem
pointing toward the Shrine and the branch and leaves projecting outward. So is represented the Shinto conception of life coming forth into
the objective universe from the subjectivity of divine spirit; and thus the
mind becomes concentrated on the truth that not only man but all existence is divinity. Respect for trees shown by Shinto has the further meaning
that the past exists through its influence on the present, for age adds to
the spiritual sensitiveness inspired by Shinto trees.

Continuity of life and life's origin in the realm of spaceless divine
spirit are emphasized by Shinto, too, through respect paid to ancestors.
Ancestors are not objects of worship in Shinto. The fundamental conception of the Shinto principle of respect for ancestors is founded on the
spirituality of mankind. The ancestral line carries the living individual
back to the initiating impetus of divine spirit. Certainly, immediate rela-
tives who have departed from earthly life are remembered with special
devotion, but the basic idea of ancestral respect is much more than that.
Ancestorship unites all life with the pure spirituality of spaceless Heaven,
whatever the evolutionary forms may have been. It is not the form that
matters but the Heavenly divine origin. This idea is expressed in a poem
taught Japanese school children:

[9] Rev. D. C. Holtom, D.D., "Some Notes on Japanese Tree Worship," *Transactions* of
the Asiatic Society of Japan, December, 1931, pp. 2, 4, 19.

Being a descendant of Taka-mi-musubi-no-Kami, it makes no difference who were my intervening ancestors.

Taka-mi-musubi-no-Kami is the mythological personification of creative growth of divine spirit originating in Heaven. Respect for ancestors, therefore, should recall to memory the first ancestor, which means life's Heavenly origin. To call Shinto a cult of ancestorship is to mistake the fundamental principle of Shinto unless this conception is understood. Shinto is a cult of ancestorship as an expression of the primaeval subconscious intuition that mankind's ancestry makes man a descendant of Heaven, which means man and divine spirit are the same. Because Shinto realizes humanity's divinity, the people of Japan regard themselves as being united in an all-inclusive family relationship; and in this sense, respect paid to the great men of the nation's past, is respect shown for ancestors of the nation considered as a vast spiritual family whose members include, as well, the Heavenly divine spirit, personalized as Kami.

Announcement of present happenings to ancestors is the way Shinto emphasizes its conception that, since the present and the past never are spiritually disunited, those who have gone before have the right to share in any responsibility for accomplishments by their descendants. Such announcements are very far from being a superstition of the past. The tradition has practical importance, for it is not just a form. It is based on a realistic understanding of man's divine origin and the continuity of human effort as the effort of divine spirit on earth. There is a sense of added responsibility when the individual realizes he is not acting entirely as a representative of present conditions but is carrying forward movements associated in various ways with his family's or the nation's ancestry. Individualism does not become self-sufficient when memory preserves the fact that the present has its obligations to the past and to Heaven, itself. Stability is given to the divine tradition in this way, which strengthens the individual and the nation. Announcement of events to ancestors further indicates that Shinto cannot hold to any theory conferring on Heavenly divinity or on the spirit of a departed individual any kind of magical power to know or to control the future. If such suzerainty over Fate were supposed to exist in the spaceless realm of divine spirit, it would be useless to inform ancestors of developments already known to them. It is an erroneous assumption that in Shinto, ancestors are deified in this matter or in any other way. To pray to ancestors or petition them as to a deity is not Shinto.

Shinto cannot be explained by any form of deism. Theistic doctrines revolve about deities who create the universe apart from themselves or who control the universe or deities demanding worship and conferring or withholding salvation and some form of desired satisfaction after death. According to Shinto, divine spirit did not make the universe, but *is* the universe. Divine spirit does not control the universe but self-creatively expands as the universe, for to control means omnipotent mechanism while to create means to generate the new. Mankind neither worships divinity in Shinto nor requires salvation at the hands of an aloof deity, for man and divinity are the same.

Divine spirit cannot be immanent in the universe by the Shinto meaning because there are not two entities, divine spirit and a universe into which divine spirit enters. A thought is not immanent in the words that objectify the thought, for thought and words are the same—subjectivity become objective—even when the thought, through lack of experience, evolves itself as ineffective words. The thought can be more than the words and can express itself contradictorily through different words; but the words cannot be different from the thought. Shinto is not idolatry for there are no holy images in Shinto either for observation or worship. Shinto is not monotheism, for it has no deity creating and ruling the universe apart from itself. Shinto is not polytheism, for it recognizes no gods. Nor is Shinto pantheistic for Shinto does not regard an omnipotent logical principle as identifying itself with the universe, but sees divine spirit as living reality self-creating itself as the universe.

Shinto did not originate with mystics for the mystic is primarily self-conscious and seeks explanations of existence by trying to move into the subconscious when surface logic fails to satisfy him. Mystics may reach the subconscious depths and realize the truth of divinity, but always the mystic returns to the self-conscious surface as an individual separated from divinity, considering himself inspired to interpret what he has found in terms of his personal environment and training. The simple truth, divined in the subconscious, becomes distorted by self-conscious efforts to give it partisan meanings. The mystic realizes the oneness of divine spirit and thereby shows the universality of the Shinto conception; but the self-conscious tendency toward separation intrudes when the mystical experience is individualized to accord with specific surface dogmas. Shinto never has followed this path, for it never has sought to explain itself. Human nature, expressing itself in instinctive actions and attitudes toward existence, is not a mystical principle, though its ways of operation are mysterious to self-consciousness. It is the same with Shinto.

Shinto, however, has a transcendental meaning in the sense that since divine spirit is the universe, it transcends any one aspect of the universe, and may extend itself in many ways not known to its three dimensional manifestations. Shinto is not transcendental, however, in any meaning that implies there is an original maker of the universe who produces the universe and at the same time is superior to the production. Man transcends his first efforts by competence to expand in versatility of action; but his efforts and himself are the same. Shinto sees divine spirit as humanity and yet more than humanity, for divine spirit is all-inclusive. Yet, this fact does not make man any less than divine spirit. In other manifestations, divine spirit has itself become less than humanity, but however the difference may be expressed and whatever form it may take, the "less than humanity" is divine spirit just as mankind is divine spirit.

Divine spirit, in Shinto, transcends any of its individual self-expressions, for if this were not so, the conception of expanding creative power would disappear. The divine creative impetus must have limitless possibilities of self-development and so is transcendental, being both spatial and non-spatial, subjective and objective, subconscious and self-conscious. In its objective expansion, divine spirit creates entirely new activities, desires and environments. At the same time, its creative competence transcends these movements of itself and is more than them. But, to conceive the "more" as being a static, Changeless All, is not Shinto, for to be changeless in this sense is to include absolutism and omnipotence; but Shinto rejects any principle which elevates the static above the creative.

Shinto shows a strongly felt subconscious intuition that beside the individual expressions of divine spirit there is co-ordination of divinity. Unification, however, is carefully suggested so that there shall be no destruction of individual creative self-development. The special position in Shinto of Amaterasu, the supreme Heavenly Kami, as well as the development of this idea in the Shinto personality of the Japanese Emperor and the unique continuity of Japan's national unification under Shinto influences, all testify to the Shinto conception that divine spirit is co-ordinated in a Unified Whole. But, Amaterasu is individualistically personalized, the Emperor has his individual personality and the Japanese people are individuals. Co-ordination and individualism of divine spirit preserve their own identities, as it were, in Shinto, in the same way that the activities of any person are individualistic expressions of himself, while he is also the co-ordinating centre of them all, and grows in coordination as his activities increase.

Neither transcendentalism nor the intuition of a Unified Whole in Shinto carries any implication of Supreme Deity. The meanings are not analysed by Shinto but are primaeval conceptions that exert their influences from within the depths of subconsciousness, not in the form of creeds or ecclesiastical doctrines. Ecclesiasticism is entirely absent from Shinto, for it is a self-conscious movement formulated to satisfy surface requirements of life. Since Shinto does not express the knowledge life has of subjective reality in ways comprehensible to self-conscious requirements for explanations of existence, it is not strange that there are two attitudes toward life in the Japanese mentality, one subconscious and the other self-conscious.

Shinto is the subconscious current of life's innermost knowledge of itself and materiality, flowing ceaselessly far below the surface of the stream of human existence. It keeps the Japanese mentality attuned to the fact that humanity has Kami ancestry and all the universe is divine spirit, and it also stimulates the impetus of creative action. Neither of these subconscious influences, however, must be self-consciously felt in order to become effective. When they are self-consciously realized, the effect may be more pronounced than otherwise. But, the inherited tradition exerts much of its sway even when there are self-conscious denials of it; for in Japan the persistence of the subconscious racial intuition, originating in the country itself, is strong enough to prevent self-conscious principles of life, imported from abroad, from gaining complete dominance.

On the surface of self-consciousness, Japan has transferred from other cultures their explanations of life and of ethical principles, to satisfy the surface requirements of her own civilization. The self-conscious doctrines have been changed in some important respects, to conform to the dominance of the Japanese spirit of activity and to meet the Shinto conception that man is of divine origin; but in subconscious form, not in any analytical sense. The imported doctrines maintain their original terms of expression, but the meanings are modified in the responses that result.

These two movements exist at their different levels, each having its own sphere of influence. The national spirit is Shinto. The self-conscious explanations of life are alien. The intuitive responses of the Japanese people to great crises and the innermost feelings of the people are Shinto. The surface expressiveness is of foreign origin. The Japanese have never analysed themselves intensively, and have never evolved sufficient self-conscious awareness of the profound power that exists in Shinto to stimulate a fresh realization of the meanings of existence and to determine why it has exerted so lasting and profound an influence on the culture of Japan. The surface creeds hold sway because their explanations of existence have appeased the cry of the soul for spiritual knowledge that would give it peace in the troubled world of anxieties and bereavements.

So a Japanese may be a Buddhist or a Christian or a Confucian and also remain Shinto. He may adhere to any specific doctrine that satisfies his self-conscious requirements, or to none. At the same time he is Shinto in his subconscious responses to the divine ancestral intuition which has become his unexpressed traditional heritage from the primaeval past. The self-conscious demands of the mind differ among different individuals and change from generation to generation; but the subconscious intuition does not deviate from the primal knowledge of reality expressed in Shinto mythology. The Japanese who have never read the mythology understandingly or who have never read it at all still have the subconscious knowledge; for it has passed into the racial memory and is imbibed from infancy by training in ways of life that have become traditional without being analysed. The most characteristic traits of any race are the traditional ones that are seldom self-consciously expressed and can rarely be described by the individuals, themselves. So it is with the influence of Shinto.

Shinto never antagonizes self-conscious efforts to explain life. Antagonisms among men spring from self-conscious differences. Human conflicts always are on the surface of life among rival self-conscious doctrines or ambitions. The subconscious power of Shinto awaits the outcome, holding its steady influence below the surface of the mind, and knowing that self-consciousness can learn only by experience and experiment in accordance with objective conditions of life. Shinto must be tolerant, too, because all surface experiments of self-consciousness are themselves Shinto in the wider sense, since they are divine spirit seeking its own way. Were Shinto to become prejudiced and try to suppress arbitrarily the self-conscious search for meanings in life, Shinto would belie itself.

Japan has been stimulated and benefited mentally and morally by the self-conscious doctrines from abroad that have been given hospitality by Shinto. They have been sources of strength to scholarship and to intellectual growth and they have comforted the weak and afflicted. Those aspects of the foreign creeds containing elements of inaction and pessimism and intolerance have been at least partly overcome by the subconscious power of Shinto, influencing the Japanese spirit. Too, the spiritual and ethical creeds that have made their way into Japan to serve self-conscious needs not met by Shinto, have undoubtedly tended to preserve the pure subconsciousness of Shinto. For, if there had been no importations of alien sophistication into Japan, inevitably the Japanese would have had to develop their own self-conscious principles of life. They would have brought Shinto to the surface, explored and analysed it inadequately, at a time when self-consciousness in Japan was not fitted for such effort. Shinto would have lost its profound subconscious influence and would have gone the way of other primaeval intuitions of life, repressed by surface manipulations and replaced by self-conscious dogmas.

Shinto has remained the national cult of Japan, undefiled by surface impurities because it has been kept below the surface, for the time to ripen when it may be clarified and made more explicit without harm to its primaeval intuition. Every nation has some such saying as "All men are the same," or "There is no difference beneath the skin." This is the ideal in mankind's self-conscious relations toward which Shinto points. This spiritual meaning has always existed in Shinto, but never has been self-consciously expressed. It is beginning to find self-conscious expression however, in the West, among people who never have heard of Shinto, indicating that the Shinto conception is more than a racial one.

Over the entrance to the Riverside Baptist Church, near Columbia University, in New York City, is a central figure of Christ, around whom are grouped busts of the principal religious leaders, scientists and philosophers of all time. They include Buddha, Confucius, Plato, Aristotle and many others who lived before the time of Christ. Darwin, who rejected religion and whose doctrine of evolution was bitterly attacked by orthodox Christianity, is among the number. So is Mahomet, whose followers fought fiercely against the Christian creed and prevented the Christian Crusades from gaining possession of the Holy Land of Christ. Emerson is the only American in the group; and there is one living person, Albert Einstein, a Zionist Jew, whose race crucified Christ. It would be impossible to bring together a more representative group of opposites among men. All, however, are enshrined together at the portal of an orthodox Christian church, whose minister is Rev. Harry Emerson Fosdick and among whose members is John D. Rockefeller, Jr., the distributor of his father's vast fortune for philanthropic enterprises in every part of the world, without regard to nationality or religious beliefs.

Here, in stone, is carved an objective manifestation of the true sub-conscious intuition of Shinto. The conception of Shinto that every way of man is a way of divine spirit on earth and that antagonists are Shinto in choosing each his own manner of experimenting with knowledge, could not find a better representation. And if Shinto be accused of primitive superstition in erecting Shrines to living persons, the Riverside Baptist Church in modern America must be put in the same category for placing the bust of Einstein in its entrance Shrine, thereby emphasizing the subconscious truth that man does not have to wait for bodily death to be divine spirit. Such a pioneer movement in reinterpreting modern spirituality shows how the modern mind is returning to the subconscious intuition of primaeval man. Coming at a time when science is destroying materialistic philosophy, it shows, too, that self-consciousness can enlarge its competence to apprehend by one step further the primaeval knowledge that all the universe is divine spirit. Shinto always has held to this truth though never carving it in stone for visible understanding. Every religion of the future that seeks creative development, must eventually return to it, not as a mystical idea beyond human comprehension but as a plain statement of reality revivifying spiritual interpretations of life.

Since Shinto never has explained these meanings to self-consciousness, it has not become either a formal religion or a philosophy. Shinto has always remained a pure subconscious spiritual intuition. It is more than religion in its all-inclusive understanding of the universality of divine spirit. It is less than religion in its unresponsiveness to the requirements of self-consciousness for coherent explanations of spirituality in keeping with divine spirit's experiences in the objective world. The Shinto intuition can serve as sufficient spiritual inspiration for all who comprehend the depths of its implications; but to interpret Shinto in any orthodox ecclesiastical way separating humanity and the universe from divinity will destroy it. If the basic Shinto truth that life is divine spirit seeking self-creative progress be retained, self-consciousness can expand this meaning in various ways as knowledge increases. To teach the Shinto truth in simple forms for the enlightenment of men, on a religious basis, is certainly possible; but Shinto, itself, in its direct intuitional awareness of the universality of divine spirit and its subconscious understanding of divine spirit's self-creative development can never be confined within any theological creed.

In its denial of omnipotent deity, Shinto is not atheistic in the sense of being unspiritual. Atheism has an anti-spiritual meaning, and so it cannot serve as a weapon against Shinto, for Shinto holds that man and the entire universe are divine spirit. When Christ was accused by the Jews of committing blasphemy because he called himself the Son of God, he defended himself by asking how the Jews could bring such a charge against him when they themselves were taught by their own divine law that "Ye are gods."[10] Christ was referring to the passage in the Old Testament which states:

> I have said, Ye are gods; and all of you are children of the Most High.
> But ye shall die like men and fall like one of the princes.[11]

This utterance is pure Shinto, except that Shinto uses the word Kami, instead of "gods." In translating "Most High," however, which means Jehovah, the Shinto word Kami might be used with no inconsistency at all, for the idea of height, personalized to imply divinity, is implied in one of the meanings of Kami. The passage of the Psalms, describing men as gods—or, in Shinto, Kami—therefore might find a place in Shinto with no change in the basic idea. For, the meaning is that humanity is divine and has a Heavenly ancestry, though human beings do not live their earthly life as divine beings forever. Christianity and Judaism are not accused of being atheistic because the Psalms call men "gods." Neither, therefore, can Shinto be called atheistic, in any obnoxious or materialistic sense, because it calls all humanity Kami. Shinto is atheistic in that it does not recognize an omnipotent deity controlling the universe; but it is not unspiritual in expressing this idea. Higher than any theory of theism separating the divine from the human is the Shinto meaning that man and the divine are the same—a meaning which Christ used as his defence against the charge of blasphemy, but which has not been followed by Western theologians who have segregated man from the divine.

Shinto Shrines are not religious edifices but are places for spiritual refreshment where man renews the primaeval intuition that humanity and divine spirit are the same. Before every Shinto Shrine are entrance gateways, two upright pillars with a crossbeam on top, called torii. The form of primitive torii is like a bridge support. So, symbolically, it may be said that torii are the terminals of the mythological Floating Bridge of Heaven connecting earth and Heaven. Shinto Shrines, therefore, can be regarded as concentration centres of the Heavenly spirit where man,

---

[10] The Gospel according to St. John, Chapter X, Verses 34-6.
[11] Psalm LXXXII, Verses 6-7.

passing through the torii, communes with his divine ancestry and directs his mind to the primaeval truth that the universe is divinity. No acceptance of creeds is necessary to recall this subconscious inspiration to the self-conscious memory. Where formal religions dominate, he who does not accept a definite ecclesiastical dogma is adjudged a spiritual outcast and has no place to turn for reminders of his spiritual being in company with others. Before a Shinto Shrine, however, a bow is sufficient to retain one's spiritual self-respect. Whether it be enough to stimulate self-conscious comprehension to an adequate degree depends on the individual and the fulness of the meaning he is competent to understand. If not, then religion as an additional stimulus has its part to play.

For large numbers of people, religions will long continue to accompany progress by satisfying self-conscious yearnings for consolation, inspiration and approval by formal authority. Shinto, as a permanent, subconscious intuition, will not seek to interfere with these demands of self-consciousness as long as they exist. But, Shinto is not likely to remain forever inexpressive, for the progress of self-conscious competence to understand subconscious meanings is an invitation to Shinto to make itself more adequately comprehended without in any way departing from its primaeval knowledge of truth. Modern life requires self-conscious expansion and reconciliation of self-conscious knowledge with subconscious intuition in spiritual matters. So, Shinto can reveal, through a new self-expression, ways of modifying religion in conformity with the primal knowledge that man and divine spirit are not two. The invitation to do so cannot be long delayed, for the tendencies of modern science are beginning to approach this monistic implication of Shinto. Though science has destroyed materialism, lagging religions continue to hold to materialistic beliefs, for religions give man a body and soul as different entities and so separate humanity from divinity, thereby holding fast to dualism, which Shinto denies.

The Shinto intuition that the universe is spiritually monistic is certain to produce a profound change in religion as this truth in all its meanings becomes more clearly realized. In the past, Shinto has served the cause of civilization and progress in Japan by subconscious means. In the future, Shinto can widen its scope by better expressing the primal knowledge of life, without in any way changing it. Shinto has preserved Japan since the foundation of the nation throughout the intervening centuries when subconsciousness and inexpressiveness were predominating traits of the Japanese mind. Now, however, a new era of self-consciousness and self-expression is necessary for Japan's higher progress, and Shinto must become adjusted to it. If Shinto were to be discarded through inability to understand its fundamental truths, Japan would degenerate. For, the impetus of creative action as a spiritual force would be overwhelmed; spiritual unification as spontaneous, natural coordination of the nation would be lost, and the binding power of tradition would disintegrate, leaving Japan with no stable foundation—a ronin in the world of progress.[12]

---

[12] A ronin was a mediaeval samurai who became a wandering outcast.

CHAPTER V

EVIL AND SUSANO-NO-MIKOTO

SHINTO has no conception of evil as an infliction on man by an antagonist of divine spirit or as punishment for offenses against the will of Heaven. No warfare between light and darkness or holiness and sin in any ecclesiastical sense exists in Shinto. No tempter and no form of Satanic influences enter into the Shinto idea of human life. Wickedness exists in the world and evil acts are committed by man against man, but Shinto regards sinners as being Kami or divine spirit equally with those who lead the most austere and beneficent lives. As rain falls on the just and unjust alike, so the just and the unjust are divine spirit by the primaeval Shinto intuition of reality. This understanding of divine spirit as all-inclusive gives to Shinto a distinguishing spiritual character marking it apart from the dominant spiritual beliefs of other races. For, Shinto requires neither a Devil nor Hell to explain life spiritually.

The difference between sacred and profane has no ecclesiastical meaning in Shinto. As in normal relationships of human life there are sacred thoughts and sacred emotions, so Shinto develops sacred conceptions, as when divine spirit communes with its higher nature; but the lower nature is divine spirit just the same as is the higher nature. Divine spirit has its two natures. Divinity does not mean, in Shinto, absolute purity, for if it did, the impure would not be divine spirit and a dualistic conception would result which is not contained in Shinto mythology. Virtue and vice both characterize divine spirit. The primaeval intuition expressed in Shinto that man and divine spirit or Kami are the same makes any other conclusion impossible.

Since man is divine spirit on earth, humanity cannot have fallen from grace in a religious sense. Everything that exists is divine spirit, and however vicious, evil cannot be separated from divinity except as it vanishes when divine spirit purifies itself. Every aspect of the universe has its origin in the spaceless spirituality of Heaven. Mankind's ancestry is divine ancestry. Ancestorship never can be abrogated. Humanity's Heavenly ancestry cannot disappear regardless of earthly conduct. It is a permanent fact in Shinto. Self-conscious sensitiveness to man's divine origin, however, can be lost in the same way that a family can have an unworthy child, but always the fact of ancestry remains. There have been many misunderstandings of this elemental factor in Shinto, for it is baffling to the mind when adequate comprehension is lacking. Self-consciousness has developed the idea that divinity is perfect goodness and that man, who is always imperfect, cannot be entirely divine but must have a dual nature, partly divine and partly maleficent. The Shinto conception is wholly different. Shinto conceives divine spirit as emerging from spaceless Heaven or subjectivity into objectivity, creating its own new way by effort and experience, so that divine spirit must accept all the inflictions that temporary failure to create right ways of progress entails. Evil and sin thus are not independent qualities hovering over humanity; they mark the unsurmounted difficulties of divine spirit's own desire to create its objective expansion by venturing upon new ways of life.

Satisfactory explanations of evil as an ecclesiastical offence never have been made. Always some form of mysticism must be used to explain evil in a world made by a perfect creator deity. The enquiry into the problem of evil in the West is based on the so-called dilemma dating back to Ancient Greece and Rome: God did not want evil but could not eliminate it; or He could eliminate it but did not want to; or He neither wants to nor can He eliminate it. This impasse is due to the doctrine of deity making mankind and the universe and giving to life all of its endowments. Man is conceived as being separated from divine spirit who either could not or did not wish to make mankind perpetually virtuous. Omnipotence is regarded as all-wise and all-good so no answer is possible to the question of why an omnipotent deity who has made mankind allows humanity to suffer. In Eighteenth-Nineteenth Century Europe a philosophic answer was attempted. The conclusion was reached that the cause of evil is egoism, but without egoism there can be no antagonism and without antagonism progress is impossible. Hence evil was regarded as life's beneficent way of stimulating progress and so evil was pronounced to be an element in the development of the good. Certainly evil may expand progress, as when tyranny causes men to develop new capacities for co-ordination in suppressing tyrants. But often evil checks progress, as, for instance, when the egoistic individualism of divine spirit becomes more experienced than divine spirit's co-ordination. Modern progress, however, is becoming increasingly based on mutual benefit; and in Nature, evolution of progress often depends on an exchange of advantages, now being closely studied, called symbiosis—as bees gathering honey from flowers and fertilizing the flowers at the same time by carrying pollen from one to the other. The practical test of all ecclesiastical and philosophic explanations of evil is whether they eventually satisfy the self-conscious mind without recourse to mysticism, which they never do.

In the Orient, the problem of evil as developed in the highly intellectualistic theories of Hinduism and Indian Buddhism is based on the belief that individualism, as an inexplicable illusion of the mind, causes the individual to become separated from the Omnipotent Changeless All. The individual develops desires which emphasize his separation; and as he is but a part of the All, suffering and misery result from this division. Evil is regarded as being overcome only as man succeeds in suppressing all desires as well as his individualistic ego as preparation for being reabsorbed into the All. Even desire to do good prevents union with the All, for to do good it is necessary not only to have the desire to benefit someone else but it is necessary also to retain one's own individuality as the doer of good and to recognize the individuality of the one who is benefited. Complete elimination of every aspect of desire and individualism is the ideal.

The Old Testament myth that evil came into the world when Adam and Eve disobeyed the divine command not to eat the fruit of the tree of knowledge of good and evil, also contains the idea of separation as the cause of evil. For, in eating the fruit Adam and Eve separated themselves from Jehovah and became independent, whereafter the human race moved forward on its own responsibility.

Conceptions of separation and omnipotence thus form the basis of Western and Oriental ideas concerning the presence of evil and suffering in the world. Shinto does not approach the problem in any such way. For Shinto, there is no ecclesiastical problem of evil at all, nor can there be one. Since man and the divine are the same, there is no omnipotent deity who either can or cannot permit evil to exist; and since mankind is not separated from the divine, evil cannot be the consequence of any division between mankind and divine spirit. Every action of man is an activity of divine spirit on earth, and evil, as an ecclesiastical crime, has no meaning. Divine spirit, expanding into the objective universe, might have chosen to follow a fixed path of innocence, living in a perpetual Garden of Eden. But, such a movement would have resulted in mechanistic individualism, a garden of divine spirit as trained human animals.

The actual expansion of divine spirit, as it has taken place according to Shinto, is entirely different. It is a self-creative process whereby divine spirit self-develops a new meaning of divinity as objective life, culminating in humanity making its own way. In this evolution, hard, painful effort is necessary, and individualism often seeks the benefits of creative action at the expense of others until experience teaches that co-operation and co-ordination must be developed for the higher progress of divine spirit on earth.

Shinto declares divine spirit or Kami is both Rough Divine Spirit and Gentle Divine Spirit: Ara-Mitama and Nigi-Mitama. This conception is contrary to ecclesiasticism which imagines deity as wholly beneficent, while at the same time ecclesiasticism invests deity with characteristics of jealousy and anger, inflicting chastisement even on future generations for offences by ancestors. Shinto does not entangle itself in such perplexing conclusions, for Shinto does not see deity as omnipotent nor as Karma, dispensing benefits and devising punishments for mankind. Divinity is understood by Shinto to be self-creative, making its own way in the objective world of experience and developing rough and gentle sides during the process. Life struggling against itself is divine spirit sacrificing itself to itself, so that from the standpoint of divine spirit as a whole, there is really no sacrifice nor any evil. When an individual sacrifices himself for others, no evil is committed in terms of humanity as a whole. Soldiers, wounded in battle because of lack of experience in warfare, do not mean evil is present in the army, though the results are evil for the individual sufferers. Similarly, in life, divine spirit as a whole shows no evil when men become victims in life's struggle to progress, though individuals suffer because of the evil effects of life's lack of experience. As divine spirit gains in experience, evils gradually disappear. There would have been no progress, however, had divine spirit refrained from experimenting with new ways of advancement through fear of damaging itself. To overcome evil by retiring from the world for cloistered inaction, is not Shinto. He who refrains from progressive action in search of static divinity belies his own divine nature, according to Shinto. Omnipotence can overcome evil automatically by destroying human freedom and making humanity static machines of virtue; but creative divine spirit cannot do so for creative divine spirit seeks to expand in absolutely new ways not known in advance.

Divine spirit, self-creating a new spiritual development in the objective universe, as implied by Shinto, gives to divinity an expansive character impossible for omnipotence. Spontaneous creation of the absolutely new is beyond the power of an Omnipotent Changeless Absolute. Omnipotence includes all knowledge of the future; but what can be foreseen must be known in advance in all its aspects. The absolutely new, however, is that which cannot be foreseen nor known until it is created. Omnipotence cannot produce the spontaneously new, which is unforeseeable, for if it did, it would not be omnipotent. Creative divinity is not limited in its creativeness since it generates what cannot be foreknown. The Shinto universe of creative divinity, therefore, is a universe of limitless reality while a universe of omnipotence is limited to mechanism. In self-creating limitless reality of objective action, divine spirit encounters obstacles due to lack of experience, and these obstacles we call "evil."

The presence of evil in the world, as conceived by Shinto, does not stultify the divine nature by imposing on divinity responsibility for being able to relieve human suffering while refusing to do so. The sufferings of life are the sufferings of divine spirit in search of progress in the objective world. Cataclysms of Nature are the same, for to Shinto, all Nature is divine spirit. The most devastating inflictions Japan endures are periodic earthquakes. Shinto, however, never has conceived a malevolent Kami of earthquakes penalizing mankind. Shinto shows its loyalty to the subconscious intuition that the universe is all divine spirit in impressive manner by this fact. The temptation to self-consciousness to imagine catastrophes as being caused by divine wrath or an evil spirit are often resistless. At the time of the Lisbon earthquake, in 1755, when 30,000 people were killed, the French clergy said it was God's punishment for the sins of the people of Lisbon, an interpretation that brought a famous denunciation from Voltaire. Shinto would regard earthquakes as implying that divine spirit as Nature had not yet fully adjusted itself to desirable stabilization in the material realm. The Shinto conception of evil thus serves as a stimulus to man when he realizes that evil must be overcome or repaired by man's own efforts and it is not a Heavenly penalty to be evaded by worship.

Shinto, as a subconscious intuition, does not provide mental relief for self-conscious imaginings, for self-consciousness must relieve itself in its own ways. No moral code, as an aid to self-conscious ethical advancement, exists in Shinto. It is not true that Shinto has no moral code because the Japanese are naturally upright, and therefore need no instruction in principles of conduct. The Japanese have splendid standards of life but so have other people. Every country, however, has its immoralities and unethical ways. If the Japanese were exceptions, there would be no necessity for criminal laws and courts of justice in the country nor for government supervision over "dangerous thought." Shinto conceives divinity in Heaven as having rough divine spirit and gentle divine spirit and there are various episodes related in Shinto mythology that show benevolence and right conduct have not always been in the ascendant. Since the Heavenly divine spirit at times has allowed its rough side to become too rough, it is impossible to maintain, as some Japanese commentators have tried to do, that the natural character of the Japanese made a primaeval code of morals unnecessary.

The primary reason why Shinto has no moral code is because Shinto is a direct subconscious intuition of the primaeval mind, while moral codes are made by self-consciousness after the self-conscious mind has reached a comparatively high stage of development. Shinto has always been a subconscious power in Japanese culture and it has never undertaken expansion in terms of any profound self-conscious expression. Moral codes arise out of the analytical processes of the mind; but Shinto is not analytical and does not generalize. Offences against neighbours are condemned by Shinto as are various kinds of impurities, but fixed moral regulations were not included in Shinto mythology. Kamo Mabuchi, writing in the Eighteenth Century a defence of Japanese morality, said:

> It has been alleged that as the Japanese had no names for "benevolence," "righteousness," "propriety," "sagacity" and "truth" they must have been without these principles. But these things exist in every country, in the same way as the four seasons which make their annual rounds. In the spring, weather does not become mild all at once, or in the summer, hot. Nature proceeds by gradual steps. According to the view of the Chinese, it is not spring or summer until it becomes mild or hot all of a sudden.[1]

That is to say, moral ideas evolve as gradual processes and are not suddenly devised in advance of human experiences. In primaeval Japan, ethical principles unquestionably must have lagged behind Chinese standards because the Chinese became sophisticated and self-conscious while Shinto remained inarticulate. The welcome given by Japan to Buddhism and Confucianism testifies to this fact. An impetus on the surface of the mind was necessary to stimulate ethical development in Japan. When Ninigi descended from Heaven to earth he was given a Mirror, Sword

---

[1] Quoted by Sir Ernest Satow, op. cit.

and Jewel as ethical and spiritual symbols; but no definite instructions went with them. None could have been given, for Ninigi represents divine spirit itself emerging into objectivity for self-creative development. The conditions to be created could not be known in advance, and so self-consciousness of divine spirit had to be left to devise its own moral principles to meet the new situations that were to be generated. Ninigi was told to look into the Mirror to see reflected the Heavenly divine spirit—a superb conception in its perpetual reminder that man and divine spirit are the same; and meaning, too, that man must look within himself, not to Heaven, for the spiritual impetus of self-development. But, self-consciousness had to evolve before morality could become expansive; and Japan reached to the continent of Asia for this power under the creative impetus of Shinto that keeps the Japanese mind always open for progressive ideas.

This does not mean Shinto is destitute of ethical influences. They are subjective, however, not self-consciously analysed, and they need self-conscious understanding to become fully effective.

> The recognition of the fact that there is love for mankind in the warmth and light which proceeded from him (Amaterasu, the Sun Kami) was a truly magnificent idea in a world destitute of religion.[2]

The warmth and light are shared by all, good and bad, for all humanity, as well as Amaterasu are divine spirit, in Shinto. But, this primaeval understanding requires explanation that Shinto has not given, though subconsciously it has influenced the alien ethical codes in Japan. Ecclesiastical ethics imply that man is naturally sinful and cannot develop moral principles unless he is instructed by Heaven or an aloof deity. Shinto holds man is neither naturally sinful nor naturally good, but is divine spirit on earth seeking self-development and creative action in new ways, and in the course of this evolution, experience and inexperience lead to good results as well as bad results. In this sense Shinto is pragmatic. The Mirror, Sword and Jewel given to Ninigi are pragmatic symbols, for they can be interpreted in many different ways according to the different experiences of individuals along the path of progress and in keeping with the versatile viewpoints the Sacred Insignia inspire. Individual responsibility is thus inculcated by Shinto. When it is realized that man is divine spirit on earth, charged with carrying forward the progress of divinity's earthly self-development, failure means individual

---

[2] W. G. Aston, *Shinto: The Way of the Gods*, p. 349.

responsibility has been neglected or shirked, with loss to the Heavenly purpose. Right action thus gains a powerful impetus.

But, right action cannot be left to subconscious sensitiveness alone, for activities are objective, and require surface understanding as well as subjective feeling, So ethical teachings have their part to play in life, which is why Japan welcomed the ethical culture of China when Shinto did not create a surface code. Yet, written codes by themselves are insufficient to produce progressively beneficial results. The written word, after a time, becomes formalized and does not inspire flexibility of responses to life's changing conditions. Only the inner sensitiveness of the creative impetus can prevent this occurrence. The association of the subconscious creative power of Shinto with the moral principles produced self-consciously on the Asiatic continent has given to Japan its ethical self-development. In China, the Confucian moral code has not been adequate to maintain virtue among the people; nor was India able to gain permanent inspiration from the formal spiritual principles of right conduct taught by Buddha. Without creative activity, spiritual and moral doctrines lose their vitality. Utilitarian development and increases in standards of living provide in themselves, for the culture of creative action, an impetus for practical morality beyond the power of ecclesiastics or written principles of ethics to stimulate. Shinto has conferred this beneficent result on Japan.

Slavery, the most immoral of all human institutions, was upheld by ecclesiastics and was condemned by no moral code in the West, until utilitarian inventions produced machines made of matter that gave more efficient results than human slave machines. Had there been no such utilitarian progress in the West, slavery still would exist there. George Finlay, the British historian, writing in 1851, said:

> The fact is that in no country where it prevailed has rural slavery ceased until the price of the productions raised by slave-labour has fallen so low as to leave no profit to the slave-owner. . . . History affords its testimony that neither the doctrines of Christianity nor the sentiments of humanity have ever yet succeeded in extinguishing slavery where the soil could be cultivated with profit by slave-owners. No Christian community of slaveholders has yet (i.e., to 1851) voluntarily abolished slavery.[3]

---

[3] *History of Greece from the Crusaders to the Turks*, p. 197.

In Japan, where there was no native code of morals, "the sale and purchase of human beings" was finally forbidden in the year 1699[4] at a time when Western nations, with minutely detailed codes of morals, were sending expeditions to Africa to seize the native blacks and sell them in slave markets under the most revolting and barbarous conditions. It is not, therefore, to a code of morals that we must always look for enlightenment concerning the practical ethical altitudes of a country.

When moral codes are regarded as being divinely inspired by a deity separated from mankind, they are usually utilized by ecclesiastics as sacred laws, carrying grave Heavenly penalties if broken. Shinto has prevented the Japanese mentality from being seriously troubled by such ideas that terrify believers who give to the priesthood the right to determine what shall happen to man after death. These foreign notions introduced into Japan have been made largely innocuous, for fear of divinity does not enter into the Shinto conception. There can be no dread of the wrath of an aloof deity when all humanity is itself divine spirit.

> The saying of the old Roman poet that "Fear first made the Gods," does not hold good for Shinto. It is rather . . . inspired by love and gratitude more than by fear. . . . Their worshippers come before them (the Shrine Kami) with gladness, addressing them as fathers, parents or dear divine ancestors, and their festivals are occasions of rejoicing.[5]

If there were any sacrilege in Shinto, it would be considered sacrilegious to believe that Heavenly divine spirit—the divine parent—damns human beings and sends them to purgatory or hell. Divine spirit cannot damn itself nor send itself to hell for venturing forth into new fields of creative action where success and failure in human relationships as well as in material productivity are relative to divine spirit's accumulated knowledge and experience. The conception that man must endure torment after death for life's failures and for not accepting some fixed ecclesiastical creed never occurred to the primaeval Shinto mentality. It is an invention of self-conscious ecclesiasticism trying to terrorize mankind into acceptance of priestly control over the human soul. Those who continue to accept the doctrine of hell fire have no right to look down upon such simple superstitions as have at times crept into the surface manifestations of Shinto. No primitive superstition ever has debased humanity as has the superstition of a deity imposing damnation

---

[4] Brinkley, *op. cit.,* p. 174.

[5] W. G. Aston, *Shinto* (in Religions Ancient and Modern Series), p. 7.

on human beings and condemning them to perpetual torture for disobeying injunctions of organized religions. Original sin is foreign to Shinto. Were such a doctrine to find a place in the Shinto conception, it would mean divine spirit had condemned itself to separation from its own all-inclusive divinity, which is impossible. The absence of a sense of ecclesiastical sin from Shinto has had the wholesome effect of preventing morbid reactions that frequently overwhelm the self-conscious mind when it has been taught that offences have been committed against a distant deity who passes sentences on sinners:

> One of the characteristics that specially interested me in the Japanese temperament was the relative absence of sense of sin. . . . I was particularly struck, when discussing insanity with Professors Imamura and Miyake, to learn that delusions of a religious nature with sense of guilt, so common in this country (England) are practically absent in Japan.[6]

There is a true conception of parenthood in the Shinto idea of Heavenly divinity, not a misinterpretation based on a false conception of Heaven as the omnipotent maker of man; and it is this primaeval idea that causes Shinto to keep the self-conscious mind clear of a vindictive god seeking to magnify himself by punishing sinners. Absent from Shinto, too, are pharisaism, bigotry, fanaticism, cant and other similar ecclesiastical characteristics which disappear when it is realized that Heavenly parentage means man and divine spirit are one.

Since Shinto has no principle of ecclesiastical sinfulness separating man from divinity, it is impossible for man to be lost, in any religious meaning. To be lost means to be separated. Souls never are lost in Shinto and so cannot be saved. Humanity has not been cast adrift by Heaven, according to Shinto. Divine spirit has come forth from the subjectivity of Heaven into the objective universe intent on creating new self-development, but the self-conscious ecclesiastical mind, in perplexity, has considered itself thus separated from subjective reality, thereby causing the idea that man and the divine are different entities. Shinto, however, which has never become analytically self-conscious, has not fallen into this error and so has not had to develop any conception of salvation for mankind nor evolve any principle of man and the divine

---

[6] C. G. Seligman, M. D., "Japanese Temperament and Character," *Transactions* of the Japan Society (London), Vol. XXVIII, pp. 131-2.

becoming divided through man's sinfulness. Shinto's dominant emphasis falls not on a return of mankind to an original Heavenly home of divine spirit, but on divine spirit advancing more and more into the world of objective reality. So, for Shinto, "progress and redemption are the same."[7] By progress, however, is meant not only material advancement, but also self-development of the divine personality in its human form.

Though Shinto does not accept any principle of ecclesiastical sin or divine salvation for humanity, this does not mean Shinto sees no difference between good and bad. Divine spirit can go astray, and frequently does so; but it is then for divine spirit to recall itself to right ways of conduct and activity. Divine spirit, in individualistic form, is responsible for checking the evil activities of other divine spirit. Shinto understands that both goodness and evil are possibilities to divine spirit in its own self-creative world when obstacles are encountered that are not immediately overcome. What is right and what is wrong often are controversial matters, and Shinto trusts to experience and experiment eventually to show mankind the difference between the two, for divine spirit is creative and the creative impetus does not permanently rest before any problem until it finds the correct solution. "Divine spirit must struggle individualistically and in co-ordination to create its redemption through progress, without being able to know in advance the good and the bad until after they have stood the test of experience. Shinto does not give humanity absolution when evil deeds are committed, but requires that man overcome evil by his own efforts. Absolution results in Shinto only when evil is suppressed by progress. That is the meaning of the Shinto principle that "progress and redemption are the same." The absence of a sense of sin and of salvation from Shinto, in their religious meanings, implies that there can be no Heavenly forgiveness for a fault when followed merely by verbal contrition. There is no confession of sins in Shinto for the purpose of overcoming their evil consequences.

Guilt is a personal matter in Shinto, and does not disappear through ecclesiastical rites. Purification ceremonies in Shinto do not relieve an offender from responsibility for penalizing himself for misdeeds. They give to self-consciousness power of concentrating on the spiritual divinity of the individual, but they do not wipe out the obligation to make amends. Far more frequently than other peoples, the Japanese inflict punishments on themselves. In Shinto, the individual feels himself accountable for

---

[7] Professor Katsuhiko Kakehi has made this translation of the Shinto word *Iyesaka* for the author.

acts that result wrongfully, even though he may have put forth his best efforts to attain right results. Under the influence of the Shinto tradition of responsibility, parents often penalize themselves for offences of their children, and high officials for the mistakes of their subordinates. Divine spirit judges itself thus rigorously in Shinto.

Japanese history has innumerable examples of such self-judgments and high honour is paid in Japan to individuals who have not flinched even from imposing on themselves the death penalty when they have thought their faults required such expiation. Indeed, the sense of individual responsibility is frequently carried to an extreme in Japan, but it has a salutary effect that modern indifferentism may well study.

Under modern conditions of life, there is increasing insistence that the individual be entitled to privacy in his beliefs. Shinto sustains this principle but links with it insistence that responsibility be assumed for the consequences. If a private belief turns out to be wrong and results in activities that are harmful in any way, the individual, under Shinto, must inflict judgment on himself, though there be no legal penalties to cover his derelictions. Certainly there are many in Japan who have become so modernized that they do not follow the old tradition of stern responsibility; but there are more who do—and one reason why a revival of the ancient spirit of Japan is so strongly advocated in the country is to recall to the people the necessity for self-responsibility.

Shinto does not encourage the scapegoat doctrine for expiating offences by sacrificial forms. There is no evil spirit in man to be exorcised, according to Shinto. The Ara-Mitama, the Rough Divine Spirit of Shinto, must see to its own punishment when it becomes too rough; and at the same time, it must submit to the judgment of others and accept penalties imposed when public offences are committed. Divine spirit retains its self-respect by accepting punishment; for it knows that evil is the consequence of its own inexperience in the objective world and must be penalized when necessary to force efficiency to develop. At the same time, the subjective spirit, within, is not defiled by the objective evils. The mediaeval Japanese custom of *hara-kiri* is based on this fact. The disembowelling act, before an assembly, was to show that regardless of the material offence, the subjective divine soul would come forth from the body symbolically, to show publicly that it had not become contaminated. In this ceremony is represented the Shinto concept that from the standpoint of divine spirit as a whole, there is no evil, but only the appearance of it due to divine spirit seeking progress at its own expense.

Pessimism vanishes when such a principle is substituted for the doctrine of original sin:

No pessimist could profess pure Shinto. The doctrine is optimistic; and whoever has a generous faith in humanity will have no fault to find with the absence of the idea of implacable evil from its teaching.[8]

The original idea of evil appears in Shinto mythology centering about the personality of Susano-no-Mikoto, whose father was Izanagi and whose sister was Amaterasu. Probably there was a historical personage, dimly recalled by the primaeval Japanese racial memory, forming part of the basis for the Susano myth. Susano may have had associations with Korea in prehistoric times when Korea and Izumo in western Japan were in some kind of relationship, for tradition in Izumo, where the memory of Susano is highly honoured, carries this suggestion. He also had an association with the ancient Kii district of central Japan. According to Shinto mythology, Izanagi gave birth to Susano and Amaterasu after he had fled from the Land of Yomi following his failure to persuade his dead wife Izanami to return to him. Amaterasu was given Heaven to rule and Susano was given the earth. Susano, however, angered Izanagi by wishing to bid good-bye to Izanami in the Land of Yomi before departing for earth; and he roused the suspicions of Amaterasu when he desired to meet her to say farewell.

To disclose Susano's real intentions, it was agreed that he and Amaterasu should engage in a child-breeding contest. If Susano produced sons, he was to be adjudged innocent, if daughters, guilty. The myth relates how Amaterasu gave to Susano her necklace of five hundred "Yasaka jewels," which he crunched. Susano, in return gave to Amaterasu his "ten-grasp" sword, which she likewise crunched. An apparent phallic element here enters the myth but it is not emphasized. Amaterasu produced three daughters, and Susano produced five sons. This result, by the rules of the contest, should have shown Susano was guiltless. Amaterasu, however, claimed the sons made by Susano were hers because she had given Susano her Yasaka jewels to crunch, and the daughters made by herself were Susano's because she had crunched Susano's sword. The tradition does not say why this reversal of the judgment was accepted, but it was. However, there must have been some objections. The most detailed account of the "trial by birth" appears in the Nihongi, which gives several versions of the tradition. One of the

---

[8] Lafcadio Hearn, *Kokoro,* p. 277.

versions, ends its account by stating:

> He (Susano) then said: "Truly I have won." . . . The children produced
> by Susano-no-Mikoto were all male children. Therefore, the Sun God-
> dess (Amaterasu) knew exactly that Susano-no-Mikoto's intentions had
> been from the first honest. . . . After this Susano-no-Mikoto's behav-
> iour was exceedingly rude.[9]

It is difficult to evade the conclusion that Susano bad been pronounced
guilty against the verdict of the trial. His subsequent "exceedingly rude"
conduct was not unnatural if he believed he had been victimized. He
damaged rice fields, became boisterous and flayed a piebald horse, and
flung the skin at Amaterasu, frightening her so that she hid herself in a
cave until she was enticed out by the comic dance that excited all the
Kami to laughter. Susano was punished by the Kami and expelled from
Heaven. He descended to Izumo where he killed an eight-headed ser-
pent that had terrorized the land, and got from its evil body the sword of
purity which he sent to Heaven as a present to Amaterasu. Susano also
began the movement for creating co-ordination on earth, which was completed by his son-in-law Okuninushi to whom Susano gave the means of
quelling Okuninushi's eighty riotous brothers.

The Susano tradition shows the primaeval mind struggling with the
idea of evil and not being misled into a conception of an evil spirit wan-
ing against Heavenly purity. Susano, though cast out of Heaven, did not
become a devil, nor did he cease to become Kami or divine spirit. Though
he was condemned by the Heavenly Kami, very high respect is paid to
his memory by calling his enshrinement place the Yasaka Shrine. The
fact that the Susano Shrine has been given this name implies that the
child-breeding contest had not dishonoured him, for otherwise the
memory of the contest would hardly have been thus associated with
Susano's spiritual memory.

Susano had his Nigi-Mitama and his Ara-Mitama, his gentle divine
spirit and his rough divine spirit. He was punished when the latter got
beyond control but the Shinto mythology did not turn him into a demon
coming to earth to tempt mankind. On the contrary, he became helpful
on earth, bearing no resentments. At Hinomisaki, in Izumo, Susano and
Amaterasu are enshrined in the same grounds, the Susano Shrine
occupying a more elevated position than the Shrine to Amaterasu. The
two have, indeed, a very close association, expressing subconscious

---

[9] This and subsequent quotations from the *Nihongi* are from W. G. Aston's translation.

meanings not entirely clarified in the mythology. The root meaning of the word "Susano" is generally interpreted as "impetuous"; and Susano has been regarded as perhaps personifying the primitive idea of storm. To an agricultural people, both the sun and storms are necessary for their crops. Without storms there would be no harvests while too violent storms ruin the harvests. Sun and storm, Amaterasu and Susano, have a relationship in this sense not inaptly described in Shinto mythology as sister and brother. Both are required to generate crops, and though storms work evil at times, yet there is beneficence in them, as well. So it is, too, with humanity. Susano can serve as a personification of human nature, impetuous, angry at being misunderstood but not vindictive, having strong family affections, generous, brave and individualistic but helping co-ordination. Shinto centers about him the subconscious conception of divine spirit both as humanity and as the Ara-Mitama and Nigi-Mitama of all Nature.

By this response to the problem of evil, Shinto saved itself from the concept of a Devil, as a malignant, independent power planting sin in the world and tempting humanity's soul. Susano rescued Shinto from the brink of Hell; and so he is properly enshrined with high honour and his memory is venerated by Shinto, in subconscious response to his true character. Had analytical ecclesiastics been at work on the Susano myth, Susano would have been turned into a Devil, thrown from Heaven to Hell for trying to gain control of divine spirit with evil intent; and this interpretation would have served ecclesiastically and detrimentally in Japan to explain evil. But, Shinto, in its loyalty to subconscious intuitive truth did not stultify its mythology in any such way.

According to tradition, Susano had a son, Omagatsumi, "Great Evil Doer"; but very little is heard of him and he is not a tempter of mankind. He can be considered a warning that impetuosity in the father may have evil effects on the offspring. To counteract Susano's evil doing son, Susano's daughter, Suseri-bime, "Forward-Princess," married Okuninushi, and helped him to overcome tests of evil devised by Susano to prove Okuninushi's character—whereafter Okuninushi beneficently pacified the land for Ninigi's descent from Heaven to create growth of co-ordinated government. But for Susano's assistance, Okuninushi must have failed.

The Susano myth represents struggle between good and evil, not as divine spirit antagonized by a spirit of evil, but as divine spirit's Ara-Mitama and Nigi-Mitama, Rough Divine Spirit and Gentle Divine Spirit, as parts of a whole not fully co-ordinated. Co-ordination comes only as the result of creative effort and experience. Shinto understands such to be the manner of life's own self-development, for every individual personality of divine spirit is Ara-Mitama and Nigi-Mitama. The struggle to adjust each to the other is divine spirit's own struggle, which self-consciousness will understand when it gains competence to attune itself to the subconscious depths of man's inalienable divinity as intuitively known to primaeval Shinto.

CHAPTER VI

SUJIN'S RENAISSANCE OF SHINTO

SHINTO did not come into existence suddenly as a completed whole. The direct subconscious intuition of reality originated in primaeval times but it grew into a fully established tradition only as expanding experiences of life were adjusted to the original inner knowledge of universal divinity and creative action. The primal Shinto realization of the universe as divine spirit expressed itself initially through recognition of self-creative divinity in Nature. The creative impetus in man had to display more power than in the very early stages of mental evolution for man to comprehend the subconscious Shinto meaning of humanity as self-developing creative spirit on earth. Mankind's tendency, even in modern times, frequently has been to belittle himself spiritually, for the human consciousness has great difficulty adjusting itself to the intuitive knowledge of reality. When the mind is in a primary stage of growth, it has an inferiority complex due to its lack of experience, its untested abilities, the oppositions it encounters in life and its misunderstanding of its own powers. Human mentality often is surprised at its own gradually evolving competence and is inclined to attribute to some form of Heavenly favour or good fortune the results of creative action that really come from its own efforts or through association with the efforts of others. All cultures have gone through this stage of misunderstanding the creative impetus of life, and the Japanese people have not been an exception.

The misunderstanding grew in the reign of the first Japanese ruler to whom the title of Emperor was given, Kamu-Yamato-Iware-Hiko, known as Jimmu Tenno, who according to the mythology, was a grandson of Ninigi and ascended the throne in 660 B.C. There is no general agreement concerning early dates in Japanese history, but Jimmu Tenno is accepted as the first Emperor. He was an aggressive general, an expansionist and a conciliator; and his disciplined creative competence resulted in the establishment of his power in Yamato, whence civilization spread throughout Japan from the centralized political source that Jimmu Tenno founded. But, attempts were made in his reign to encourage a belief that Heavenly help was extended to him in times of difficulty. The Kojiki says that while campaigning in Kumanu mountains a "cross-sword" was sent to Jimmu from Heaven, and when he accepted it, the enemy "all spontaneously fell cut down," the meaning being that they were killed even before the sword was used against them.[1] On another occasion, the Kojiki relates that a crow was sent from Heaven to guide Jimmu on one of his expeditions; but the crow led Jimmu into an ambush, unintentionally, from which he was saved only when the enemy leader was betrayed by a younger brother.[2]

Here was a primitive bent toward seeking miraculous aid from Heaven in emergency, instead of trusting to one's own competence. Instead of giving to Jimmu the credit of succeeding in his exploits by his own efforts, there was an inclination among his followers to interpret the results as having been directed by a Heavenly power. This was a drift toward the false idea of omnipotence ruling in human affairs; and while the purpose may have been to magnify Jimmu as the favoured son of Heaven, it minimized Jimmu's own creative abilities. Had such a doctrine of material help from Heaven obtained permanent control over the culture of Japan, Shinto would have been crushed by the superstition for the creative spirit of self-reliance would have disappeared. Trust in miracles means neglect of self-effort and leads to destruction. The Emperor Jimmu is honoured as the pioneer of Japanese nationalism; but the frontier of full creative understanding of Shinto had not been crossed in his reign.

Following Jimmu came eight Emperors about whom little is known except their genealogies. The ancient records give no indication of any development having taken place in their eras. There must have been some progress, but it was not of sufficient importance to have found a place in tradition. The creative impetus was still floundering and Shinto had not turned the Japanese mentality toward full self-reliance and self-trust. Belief in miracles had not been overcome, for in the reign of the seventh Emperor after Jimmu, in the Third Century, B.C., a Chinese Taoist, Hsu Fuh, visited Japan seeking an elixir of perpetual youth, according to Japanese tradition, and his tomb still exists at Shingu in southern Kii. A movement, too, was developing to suppress the Shinto difference between the Sovereign and Amaterasu. Heavenly divinity was being removed from Heaven and lodged in the Palace. The Sacred Mirror, which had been given to Ninigi, according to the mythology, on his descent

---

[1] Chamberlain's translation, 2nd edition, p. 163 and note 6.

[2] *Ibid*, p.167.

from Heaven to earth, was meant to symbolize Amaterasu, and when Ninigi received it, he was told that be must "regard this Mirror exactly as if it were our (Amaterasu's) August Spirit and reverence it as if reverencing us (Amaterasu)."[3] Thus, from the beginning, discrimination was emphasized between the Sacred Mirror and the Sovereigns, since the latter were told to regard the Mirror as Amaterasu, herself, and to reverence it. Amaterasu personalizes the all-inclusive oneness of all divine spirit, Heavenly and earthly, according to Shinto; and to limit Amaterasu in any way, by not recognizing the superiority of all-inclusive divine spirit to any personage, is to turn from the Shinto principle. Shinto recognizes the creative power of individuals but higher than individuals is the supreme oneness of spirit. The Sacred Mirror, given to Ninigi, represented the spiritual unification of Amaterasu. But, during the reigns of the eight Sovereigns who followed Jimmu, the Sacred Mirror was losing its character as the exclusive symbol of Amaterasu, for no discrimination was being made between the Mirror and the Sovereigns, which meant no difference was understood to exist between the Sovereigns and Amaterasu. This was not Shinto. The Kogoshui, an authoritative Shinto record of the ancient traditions, says:

> In those olden days when the gods and the Sovereigns were not widely differentiated, they were wont to share the same couch, under the same roof. . . . Of old, Amaterasu-O-Mikami, symbolized by the Sacred Mirror, remained in the same house with the Emperor, so both the Deity and the Emperor were waited upon exactly in the same manner by the attendants from the beginning in Heaven, there being no discrimination between the Deity and the Sovereigns at all.[4]

The other Heavenly Kami, whose individualistic identities in the Shinto mythology represent the Shinto emphasis on individual effort, as Amaterasu represents divine oneness, were also being forgotten. The local provincial Kami of Yamato, Yamato-no-Oho-Kuni-Dama, an earth Kami symbolizing co-ordination, "Great Spirit of Yamato," had been installed in the Palace;[5] and the Nihongi says this Kami and Amaterasu

---

[3] *Kojiki*, Chamberlain's translation, p. 131.

[4] Translated by Genchi Kato and Hikoshiko Hoshimo, 3rd edition, pp. 35, 46-7. The words "gods" and "Deity" should be understood as meaning Kami. Professor Kato has informed the author that he believes the Sword given to Ninigi was regarded as symbolizing Amaterasu at that time, as well as the mirror.

[5] Dr. Ponsonby Fane in "O Yamato Jinsha" expresses the opinion that a spear symbolized Yamato-no-Oho-Kuni-Dama in the Palace. Professor Kato is of the same opinion and he has informed the author of his belief that this Kami eventually became amalgamated in popular conception with Okuninushi—the more inclusive Kami of co-ordination.

"were worshipped together within the Emperor's Great Hall." Here was
the beginning of a degenerative movement to change Shinto into a primitive religion of omnipotence on earth. Had this endeavour to make
Amaterasu and the Sovereign indistinguishable succeeded, the Palace
would have gained supremacy over Heaven in the popular mind and the
Sovereign would have been regarded as omnipotent deity on earth responsible for all human happenings. The Kogoshui says the Sovereign
and the Mirror occupied the same couch in the Palace which means
Amaterasu and the Sovereign were considered to be united as one, in an
earthly dwelling. Amaterasu is the Heavenly Ancestress of Shinto and
does not descend to earth. Amaterasu is the united whole of divine spirit,
more than individual earthly divinity. To regard the Ruler of Heaven as
not being differentiated from the Sovereign in the Palace was not only to
devitalize Shinto but also to degenerate the people. Acceptance of such a
creed has happened many times among nations in different forms, and it
has always resulted in causing the people to believe the Sovereign is an
earth god with miraculous powers. Under the influence of such doctrines the people do not put forth effort to enlarge their own creative
abilities but look to the deified Sovereign to provide for their welfare,
and so lose their competence for self-development. Shinto does not con-
fer even on Amaterasu in Heaven ability to make miracles. So much the
less could Shinto have flourished by any belief that earthly rulers have
such supernatural power.

Had the Japanese people not inherited an innate capacity for creative
action and self-development, the hesitancy in the evolution of Shinto at
this time would have been disastrous to the nation. Here was the Dark
Age of Shinto. But, the subconscious creative competence and self-confidence of the race were not crushed. The inner, intuitive power of Shinto
remained inextinguished, though largely quiescent. Rejuvenation awaited
only proper leadership to abolish the heretical principle of an omnipotent god on earth. Shinto was waiting for a creative activist to come to
power who would respond to the primaeval intuition of self-development and individual effort. Amaterasu had become concentrated in the
Palace. It was necessary to break down this backward movement and
restore the people's trust in their own creative powers. The true Shinto
conception that every individual has Heavenly Kami ancestry and should
strive to advance the cause of progress as a divine activity, had to be
emphasized. Amaterasu had to be restored to her position as universal
divine spirit while the people had to be shown that human advancement

is due to human effort and not to omnipotence. Japan required a Renaissance of Shinto to emerge from the Dark Ages.

The leader was found in the tenth Emperor, Mima-ki-iri-biko-iniwe, known by his posthumous title of Sujin, "Respecter of the Kami." To respect the ancestral Kami means to show respect to Heavenly divine spirit and not to monopolize the source of spiritual unification in one's own person; and by respecting the Kami Sujin terminated the drift toward omnipotence in primitive Japan. He carried the nation out of the Dark Ages, separated the Sovereigns from dwelling under the same roof with the Mirror of Amaterasu and demolished the principle that there is no discrimination between the Ruler of Heaven and the Sovereigns on earth. Sujin came to the throne, according to the ancient records, in 97 B.C. and reigned sixty-seven years—the most fruitful period for Shinto in the history of Japan. Sujin was Shinto's greatest known genius. He had high originality of mind, intensity of will, did not fear to try new paths of progress and possessed the rare ability of being able to distinguish between rebellion due to economic distress that required compassionate changes in policy and rebellion due to defiance of his rule that had to be suppressed. He was the first humanist among the Japanese Sovereigns. Soon after mounting the throne, he issued a decree, according to the Nihongi saying:

> When our Imperial Ancestors assumed the Supreme Rank, was it for the benefit of themselves alone? It was doubtless in order that they might thereby shepherd men and regulate the Empire. . . . Our Ministers and Functionaries, should you not co-operate in all loyalty in giving peace to the Empire?

Sujin did not seek his own benefit through continuing the policy of regarding the Sovereigns as sharing the same couch with Amaterasu. He sought to benefit the people by showing them examples of putting forth human effort to improve material conditions for the nation's welfare. The first mention in Japanese history of education, a census, organized taxation, development of transportation, shipbuilding, improving methods of agriculture all occur in the reign of Sujin. Certainly, there must have been previous primitive activities in some of these directions, but the most effective advances were made under Sujin's leadership. The Nihongi's account of his reign contains such references as the following:

> The Emperor proclaimed to the company of Ministers: "For the guidance of the people, the first thing is education."

A census of the people was begun.

Taxes were imposed anew. These are called the men's bow-end tax and the women's finger-end tax (that is, a tax on animals' skins and game and a tax on textile fabrics—the latter suggesting women had civic rights since they were assessed for taxation).

The following decree was issued: "Ships are of cardinal importance to the Empire. At present the people of the coast, not having ships, suffer grievously by land transport. Therefore, let every province be caused to have ships built."

The following edict was issued: "Agriculture is the great foundation of the Empire. It is that upon which the people depend for their subsistence. At present the water of Hanida, of Sayama in Kahachi is scarce and therefore the peasants of that province are remiss in their husbandry. Open up, therefore, abundance of ponds and tunnels and so develop the industry of the people."

Desiring to nominate a Crown Prince by test of merit, the Nihongi says Sujin asked his two sons to dream dreams—doubtless meaning they were to consider overnight their conceptions of sovereignty. Both said they had dreamt that they had ascended Mount Mimoro. The elder added: "Turning to the east eight times, I flourished a sword and eight times dealt blows with a sword." The younger said: "I stretched a cord to the four quarters with which to drive away the sparrows which fed upon the grain." Sujin passed over the belligerent elder brother and made the younger one Heir Apparent, for he wanted peace and industrial progress, not warfare for Japan.

Sujin's mentality was essentially practical. He was not an aloof monarch, sequestered and without knowledge of human nature. He was a cheerful, natural man, stern when necessary, but jovial and companionable as well. Sujin was made poetic and musical by sake and was not restrained by his rank from merry association with congenial company. The Nihongi describes an all-night party at which, when morning came, Sujin sang:

> The Hall of Miwa
> (Of sweet sake fame)
> Even its morning-door
> I would push open;
> The door of the Hall of Miwa.

The Nihongi adds that the door was thrown open "and the Emperor proceeded on his way." Such humanistic competence to relax in agreeable company, however, was associated with sternness when events required punitive measures. The Nihongi records a proclamation by Sujin ordering military action against outlying areas where the natives resisted his progressive sway:

> The distant savages do not receive our calendar because they are yet unaccustomed to the civilizing influence of our rule. We will, therefore, select some of our company of Ministers and despatch them to the four quarters so that they may cause Our Will to be known.

This expedition is called the campaign of the Shido Shoguns, "Commanders-in-chief of the four circuits" or provinces. Its importance lies not only in the success of the expedition but also in the evidence of Sujin's genius for encouraging individualistic action and self-responsibility and his recognition of the necessity for local autonomy as the way of progress.

> The leaders chosen for this task were all members of the Imperial family. . . . The Yamato armies at that remote epoch marched hundreds of miles through the country in the face of an enemy. . . . Some kind of permanent control was essential, and there is collateral evidence that the descendants of the four princely generals, during many generations, occupied the position of provincial magnates. . . . It seems justifiable to conclude that the first great impetus to that kind of decentralization was given by Sujin's despatch of the Shido Shoguns.[6]

Sujin's action in thus authorizing autonomous provincial government was due to the same fundamental characteristic of his creative genius that had caused him to destroy the doctrine of Amaterasu residing with the Sovereigns in the Palace. Sujin was a spiritual as well as a political decentralist. As long as the Divine Mirror remained in the Palace and no difference was made between the Sovereigns and Amaterasu, the idea of centralized omnipotence on earth was sure to make its demoralizing way deeper and deeper into the popular mind. Sujin declined to exercise autocratic sway over the provinces subjugated by his four generals, and allowed them freedom for self-development, though they remained coordinated through Sujin's personality as Sovereign. Guided by the same creative instinct of self-development, Sujin had previously taken measures to end the belief in Amaterasu as an autocratic earth ruler, and so

---

6 Brinkley, *op. cit.*, pp. 79-80.

restored to Japan the Shinto creed of humanity's self-creative rule on earth, co-ordinated spiritually in Amaterasu's Heavenly personality of divine oneness. The unprecedented advance in the spirit of Japanese culture which Sujin initiated was due to the subconscious Shinto intuition of reality working in his mind at a time of grave peril in Japan's internal relations. Disastrous events threatened the nation soon after Sujin came to power, but they served only to stimulate his creative genius. In the fifth year of his rule, the Nihongi relates that "there was much pestilence throughout the country and more than one-half of the people died." In the sixth year, "the people took to vagabondage, and there was rebellion, the violence of which was such that by worth alone it could not be assuaged." Here was a crisis of the utmost gravity for "by worth alone" it could not be overcome. "By worth alone" means omnipotence. It means that the worthiness of the Sovereign was unable to stem the pestilence, vagabondage and rebellion. The Kogoshui explains that no discrimination was made between the Sovereign and Amaterasu. So, "by worth alone" Amaterasu had not rescued the nation. The phrase being used at this time means the people had looked to the Palace in the past to keep the nation from disaster "by worth alone"; but the people now were distrustful of such power, for conditions were constantly becoming worse. Sujin was not the type of ruler to sit back before so dire an emergency and let events take their own course. He, too, realized that "by worth alone" the people's self-confidence and disciplined spirit could not be regained.

The Nihongi says that:

> Therefore, rising early in the morning and being full of awe until the evening, the Emperor requested punishment of the Gods (Kami) of Heaven and Earth.

This statement, however, is not Shinto, for Shinto never has contained the principle that the Japanese Sovereigns should invite punishment for national disasters. That has been the custom in China; and the author of the Nihongi who put the ancient Shinto tradition into writing in the Eighth Century, was led astray by a Chinese notion. Doubtless, however, there was a tradition that Sujin had spent a full day from early morning until evening during the crisis communing with himself—probably many days—after it had become apparent that "by worth alone" the disasters could not be assuaged. Sujin's creative powers were working within him and he naturally would have given deep thought to new steps that had to be taken to restore tranquility.

The Sacred Mirror, and the Sacred Sword which also was kept in the Palace, had shown no magic ability to overcome the distressful conditions, and the Kogoshui says Sujin "began to feel uneasy at dwelling on the same couch and under the same roof" with them. Since "by worth alone" the omnipotent divine spirit supposed to dwell in the Palace was not coming to the people's relief, it was essential publicly to acknowledge that the doctrine of "worth alone" no longer could be trusted. Action of some kind was necessary to divert the people's minds from further reliance on spiritual omnipotence in the Palace. After his day "full of awe" Sujin took his revolutionary step. He ordered the Mirror and Sword removed from the Palace and so destroyed forever in Shinto the creed that human events are controlled "by worth alone." Sujin broke with the false doctrine of omnipotence and made himself the nation's leader of creative self-development. The Kogoshui, describing the act, says:

> Whilst reigning at the Mizukaki Palace in Shiki, the Emperor began to feel uneasy at dwelling on the same couch and under the same roof beside the Mirror sacred to Amaterasu-O-Mikami and the Divine Herb-Quelling Sword, and being greatly overwhelmed by their awe-inspiring divine influence, His Majesty ordered his daughter Toyosuki-no-Mikoto to remove these Sacred Objects to Kasanui Village in Yamato Province and there establish a new holy site or enclosure, planting sacred trees and setting up sacred stones, in order to enshrine these Divine Emblems.[7]

Sujin's purpose was not to make himself superior to Amaterasu by removing the symbols of the Heavenly Ruler from the Palace. His intention was to restore Amaterasu to her rightful Shinto position as the Heavenly centre of spiritual unification and to suppress the idea that "by worth alone" divine spirit could relieve humanity from the necessity for developing self-effort. He sought, too, to give back to the Japanese people their ancestral relationship with Heavenly divinity and to emphasize afresh their own responsibilities to divine spirit.

> When the first Emperor installed the Sacred Insignia in the Palace where he himself dwelt, the instinct of filial piety and the principle of ancestor worship were scarcely distinguishable. But as time passed and the age of the Kami became more remote, a feeling of awe began to pervade the rites more strongly than a sense of family affection.[8]

---

[7] *Op. cit.*, p. 36.

[8] Brinkley, *op. cit.,* p. 79.

That is to say, to the time of Sujin, the increasing tendency was to forget that Shinto means man and Kami are the same and that there is a filial relationship between Heavenly divine spirit and humanity. Spiritual separation between man outside the Palace and divine spirit residing in the Palace was developing, which is not Shinto. Sujin ended this movement, and in doing so he recovered the primaeval Shinto principle that there is ancestral relationship not only between the Sovereigns and Amaterasu but also between all the Japanese people and the Heavenly divine spirit. It was natural, therefore, that when the Sacred Emblems were removed from the Palace there should be great popular rejoicing. The Kogoshui says "all the courtiers were present and entertained throughout the whole night at a consecrated repast."[9] They sang a gleeful song whose archaic words in the Kogoshui have been variously translated:

> What a delightfully happy evening this grand banquet gives us courtiers, who at the Ceremony of the Removing of the Divine Insignia greatly enjoy ourselves throughout the whole night! Oh, how auspicious is the snow scene this night!

> We courtiers present at the Ceremony of the Removal of the Divine Insignia now enjoy great pleasure at the grand banquet throughout the whole night in the fine sacred Yuki Hall.

> Let us courtiers make merry the whole night through! Oh, how fine for us courtiers is the sacred sake drink! What a fine long robe each courtier wears at the Ceremony of Removing the Sacred Insignia; it reaches below the knees![10]

The restoration of Amaterasu to her Heavenly seat, the abandonment of the doctrine that there was no discrimination between Amaterasu and the Sovereign, the suppression of: the growing belief in an omnipotent power controlling the nation's destiny, the recovery of the original Shinto creed that makes the Sovereigns and Amaterasu the same, in air ancestral sense, and unites the nation with divine Heavenly spirit were thus received by popular acclaim. The song of the courtiers may be interpreted as the Shinto hymn of creative freedom. The approval of subsequent generations is shown by the fact that when the Kogoshui was written eight centuries after, the song was still being sung in the following version:

---

[9] *Op. cit.,* p. 37.

[10] *Ibid,* pp. 73-4, critical note 74.

What a fine long robe each courtier in the suite wears at the Ceremony of the Removing of the Divine Insignia! Oh, how splendid is the procession to the Divine Insignia![11]

The reformation which Sujin had undertaken was not completed, however, by removing the Sacred Insignia. Calamities continued and the Nihongi says Sujin was informed by a divination that he should recognize the spirit of Okuninushi, who had consolidated Izumo in the mythological age. Having enshrined Amaterasu, Sujin was turning to other great names in the mythology. That Okuninushi was the first to have attracted him was natural, for Okuninushi was the first great creative activist among human beings in Shinto mythology. Political reasons, too, may have played a part in Sujin's desire to restore Okuninushi to national respect, to strengthen the ties between Yamato and Izumo. The Nihongi says that after Sujin recognized Okuninushi, "he also divined that it would be unlucky to take advantage of this opportunity to worship the other Gods." This statement indicates that the other Shinto Kami as individualized creative spirit had been neglected to the time of Sujin, and that Sujin was considering their restoration to a place of respect in the popular mind, thereby recognizing divine creative spirit in personalized forms. The fact that a divination was made against this intent shows some opposition was developing, for the pestilence had not disappeared. But, Sujin was not deterred. He did not trust divinations that were not in accord with his own intentions, for three months afterward, the Nihongi says:

> He divined that it would be lucky to worship the other Gods. So he took the opportunity of separately worshipping the assemblage of eighty myriads of Deities. He also settled which were to be Heavenly Shrines and which Earthly Shrines and allotted land and houses for the service of the Gods. Whereupon the pestilence first ceased; the country at length had peace; the five kinds of grain were produced and the peasantry enjoyed abundance.[12]

The rejuvenation of Shinto was now accomplished. Sujin had crushed the false creed of omnipotent, deity on earth by removing the Divine Insignia from the Palace; he had restored Amaterasu to Heaven by her

---

[11] *Op. cit.,* pp. 74-5, critical note 75.

[12] "Gods," "Deities" and "worship" are Aston's translations. They are inaccurate, for they do not have the meaning in Shinto that is given them by religious usage. The word "Kami" should have been retained instead of "Gods" and "Deities," and "paying respect to" should be substituted for "worship."

enshrinement as the divinity of the united whole; he had prevented omnipotence being associated with Amaterasu in Heaven by recognizing creative divine spirit in the ancestral individualities of other Kami. Sujin was favoured by the happy coincidence of the pestilence working itself out at the conclusion of his reforms; but the restoration of spiritual self-respect and the stimulus of self-confidence among the people played a part too, in stemming the nation's calamities, as mental invigoration and leadership to new activities always do. Not Fate, but persistent action gave Sujin success. When further disasters followed the removal of the Divine Insignia from the Palace, Sujin did not become frightened and restore them to the Sovereign's couch. When he turned to Okuninushi and conditions were not bettered, still he did not hesitate. When it was divined he should not recognize the individualized personalizations of all the Kami he ordered another divination. He continued his forward movement to the desired end. And if fortune favoured him by terminating the pestilence, fortune in the end usually favours the leader of a great progressive movement who is not held back by timid advisers pointing pessimistically to time's delays. Sujin took two years resurrecting Shinto and making himself the first ruler in history to have voluntarily separated himself from a false notion of godhead on earth after it had become a tradition associated with the Throne. His renunciation of Heavenly absolutism on earth replaced artificiality with realism, and restored to the Japanese nation the creative impetus of Shinto.

While Sujin reigned in Japan, Julius Caesar ruled Ancient Rome. The two monarchs took opposite turnings at the crossroad of life. Sujin renounced the tradition that was tending to make the Japanese Sovereigns earth deities. Julius Caesar ordered statues to be erected to himself as Jovian God on earth, and the people of Rome bowed before his self-conferred omnipotence. Japan has followed ever since the path marked out by Sujin, developing her creative powers and competence to expand progress. Rome followed the way of Julius Caesar and lost her creative instincts as the people's self-respect and sense of responsibility became polluted. Japan has attained increasing greatness from Sujin's time to the present day. Rome declined from the time of Julius Caesar and now is but a memory. Sujin turned Japan toward creative action by stimulating self-trust and self-effort. Julius Caesar turned Rome toward mechanism through belief in omnipotent power. Always in human history these two paths have been open for life to follow. Always self-responsibility has led away from omnipotence toward progress, and always belief in omnipotent control over mankind has caused debasement and deterioration.

Sujin did not separate the divine from the human when he removed the Sacred Insignia from the Palace. He separated the spurious conception of omnipotence from humanity. He restored the idea of an all-inclusive divinity to Japanese culture. He crushed the tradition that was limiting divinity on earth to the Palace and by doing so he destroyed the creed of spiritual absolutism and regenerated the Shinto principle of spiritual self-creativeness. That so vital a step for human welfare should have been taken in primitive Japan at a time when the highly civilized Ancient Romans were destroying themselves by making their rulers empty omnipotent indicates the depths of Shinto's intuitive knowledge of reality and the subconscious understanding of it that dwelt in Sujin's genius.

Twelve centuries later, Yoritomo showed the Shinto intuition was guiding him somewhat similarly when he separated the political capital of Japan from the spiritual capital. In Yoritomo's time, the politicians were trying to acquire omnipotence for themselves by ruling the nation autocratically under the shadow of the Throne. Sujin removed omnipotence from the Palace; but the politicians later sought to restore it within the political environs of the Palace for their own self-indulgence by the false claim that they were the autocratic spokesmen of the Sovereign's will. Had the tendency become permanent in Japanese culture, the nation would have reverted to the basic condition existing before Sujin's time, though with omnipotence being usurped by the courtiers around the Throne. The intuitive creative power of Shinto which saved Japan, through Sujin, from the creed of omnipotence in the Palace, likewise saved Japan, through Yoritomo, from omnipotence in political government. So, Yoritomo may be called the political reflection of Sujin.

The tributes paid to Sujin by his contemporaries show how his genius was recognized in his lifetime. The Kojiki says:

> So, in praise of this august reign, they said: "The Heavenly Sovereign, Mima-ki, who ruled the first land."[13]

It was the first land in the sense that Sujin's reign was the first to emerge from the Dark Age of Shinto. Sujin, too, was called by his people Hatsukuni Shirasu Sumera Mikoto, "The Sumera Mikoto Sovereign Who Founded the Nation." He founded the nation on the basis of the

---

[13] Chamberlain's translation, 2nd edition, p. 220.

creative spirit of Shinto. Sujin was the Meiji of his time. Like Meiji, Sujin faced old traditions that had to be reformed to give a new stimulus to creative action, and also like Meiji, he led Japan into new paths of self-development and progress. The famous rescripts of the Meiji era which are Japan's cornerstone of modern enlightenment, had their ancient counterparts in the rescripts of Sujin which are preserved in the Nihongi. Sujin had a modern mind in a primitive environment, and in this respect he reflected the subconscious knowledge of reality that exists in Shinto. To study Sujin's character and accomplishments is to become aware of the primaeval racial spirit of Japan that gave to Shinto its fundamental characteristics of creative self-development. Had Japan not followed the way directed by Sujin there would have been no Shinto in modern times. Shinto would have expired in the early period of Japanese history.

Sujin was essentially a decentralist. By stressing individual effort, self-trust and reliance on human effort for progress, and by recognizing all the ancestral Kami, he saved Japan from drifting into mechanism and spiritual reaction. But, there is more in the meaning of the Sumera Mikoto Sovereign than individual effort and human progress. Removing the Divine Insignia from the Palace did not impair the Japanese Sovereigns' unique Shinto position. It cleared the way for the Sumera Mikoto's restoration, in the true Shinto meaning, made possible because Sujin suppressed the false meaning.

CHAPTER VII

SUMERA MIKOTO

ALWAYS in Japanese history, individualism and co-ordination are discernible, each struggling to assert itself. Before the reign of the Emperor Sujin, there had been over-co-ordination, resulting in the danger of a creed of omnipotence getting possession of Japanese culture. Individual responsibility was declining and in Shinto the people had become forgetful of their rightful divine ancestry. Sujin was a strong individualist, putting forth effort as a pioneer to blaze a new pathway of progress. Sujin overcame the doctrine that there was no discrimination between Amaterasu and the Sovereigns. But, it was necessary to emphasize the fact that there is an indissoluble union of the Sovereigns and Amaterasu by the fact that Amaterasu is the Heavenly ancestress of the Sovereigns and that the Japanese nation is co-ordinated into a single whole through the Sovereigns' relationship with Amaterasu.

Individual effort had to be continued along the line marked out by Sujin and the people had to retain their spiritual identities as individuals, for it is by means of individual development of effort that co-ordination for material advancement results. But, at the same time, it was obligatory for the spiritual oneness of Heaven and Japan to be emphasized, for otherwise Shinto would have become spiritually individualistic losing an essential part of its primaeval intuition of divine co-ordination.

The Shinto meaning of co-ordination has caused the evolution of nationalistic unification in Japan to follow a course different from any other country's. Shinto does not separate Japan and the Japanese people from the originating creative divine spirit of Heaven. All are ancestrally one. The material and the spiritual have no real distinction. Shinto does not cause man to wait for death to become one with Heavenly divinity. Man always is the divine spirit, in his individual objective being, and always is divine spirit in his subjective unification with the divine source. This principle is vital to Shinto and is the subconscious strength of the Japanese nation. How to keep the Shinto unification concept always visible to the surface mind was Japan's problem in terms of nationalistic evolution, The problem was solved by holding to the primaeval Shinto conception of the Sovereign, which the nation was able to re-emphasize after Sujin's removal of the Sacred Insignia from the Palace.

Shinto does not regard Japan as being only a group of material islands, Japan—and in the wider implication of Shinto, the entire universe—is an objective extension of subjective creative spirit. Japan was not made by creative divine spirit; Japan is creative divine spirit become materialized. The Japanese people likewise, are creative divine spirit come forth from the Heavenly subjective origin of all creativeness. The Japanese were not made by creative divine spirit; they are creative divine spirit materialized into living objectivity. The phrase "Japan is the land of the Kami" expresses this idea. It does not mean the Japanese are a chosen race. No such implication exists anywhere in the Shinto mythology, which is limited to describing the creative extension of Heavenly divine spirit in terms of the Japanese nation because the mythology is a national history and not a world history. In no symbolic sense, but in full reality Shinto regards Heavenly divine spirit as expanding from subjectivity into the objective forms of Japan and the Japanese people. Not to understand this Shinto conception in its realistic sense means to misrepresent the nationalistic evolution of the Japanese people and their Sovereign.

Modern sophistication may regard such a belief as fantastic or at best an outgrown primitive superstition retained only as a curious tradition of the past with no modern meaning. If modern sophistication cannot discern the fundamental verity within the Shinto principle, it is because the modern mind has not yet accustomed itself to the new teachings of Western science which are pointing to a similar implication though in different phrasing. Sir Arthur Eddington thus describes what the new science is discerning as the basic material of the universe :

> I will try to be as definite as I can as to the glimpse of reality which we seem to have readied . . . the stuff of the world is mind-stuff. . . . The mind-stuff of the world is of course something more general than our individual conscious minds, but we may think of its nature as not altogether foreign to the feelings in our consciousness.[1]

If the material of the world is mind-stuff, it is originally subjective and not objective, for such is our own minds. Sir Arthur Eddington has explained elsewhere that the new science is in-deterministic and not mechanistic; so the mind-stuff is creative as well as subjective, as is

---

[1] *The Nature of the Physical World,* p. 276 ff.

likewise our own minds. It must, therefore, have come forth not by omnipotent fiat, but by its own self-creative impetus in evolving as the
objective universe and as life. It must have self-evolved as Japan—and
the rest of the material universe—and as the Japanese people—and all
other peoples and all existence in every form. Far back in primaeval
times in Japan, Shinto personalized the modern scientific idea of mind-
stuff by calling it Kami or divine spirit, becoming the universe by creative
expansion. Modern science is now beginning to catch up with Shinto,
for any use of the word "mind" suggests some of the implications of
personalism. The Shinto conception of Japan and the Japanese people as
Kami or self-creative divine spirit become objective does not, therefore,
have to defend itself against modern science; and so much the less against
modern scepticism.

We are justified in understanding that the mind-stuff of the universe,
which takes so many diverse forms, has a unified source within itself as
well as an individualistic impetus, since its nature "is not altogether foreign to the feelings in our consciousness." We feel not only our
individualities, but we feel in our consciousness the desire for union
with others even more insistently; for we abhor complete individualism.
We crave co-ordination with others, and if individualistic isolation —
complete individualism—be prolonged, it crushes the mind and is the
worst form of mental torture. Though the divine creative impetus seeks
individualistic effort, yet co-ordination, unification, oneness is more basic,
in preventing individualism from disintegrating into isolation.

Shinto personalizes the oneness of all divine spirit in the Heavenly
origin of creativeness, through Amaterasu. At the same time, from the
subjective source of creativeness, diverse creative movements, personalized in Shinto by the "eighty myriad" of Kami, seek objective expansion.
Within the centralized source these movements have individuality, according to the Shinto mythology, but there is as well the unified Heavenly
One—Amaterasu. As the "eighty myriad" of Kami objectify themselves
individualistically, so does the Heavenly One become objectified as unified oneness, by the Shinto conception. In that part of the universe which
divine spirit has self-created as Japan, the Japanese people are the individualistic embodiments of Heavenly divinity become objectified. The
Sovereign of Japan is the objectified embodiment of Amaterasu, the unification of creative divine spirit, in Japan. There is no difference in the
fact of divine Heavenly origin between the people and the Sovereign, in
Shinto. Nor is there any conception of omnipotence or a monopoly of

spirituality. The difference is between divine individualism and divine Shinto unification.

Shinto shows in indisputable ways its understanding that the Japanese people are Kami or divine spirit objectively self-creative and individualistic. The archaic Shinto word for man is *Hiko*, and for woman, *Hime*. *Hiko* means male being of the sun and *Hime* means female being of the sun. Amaterasu is the Sun Kami Ruler of Heaven, and man and woman, called beings of the sun, are thus given by Shinto a "Heavenly nationality."

Another Shinto word for the Japanese people is *Mikoto*. *Mi* is the Heavenly title meaning divine, and *Koto* means thing, or in this sense, being. *Mikoto* means, therefore, divine being or one having a Heavenly origin. *Mikoto* is used also in the Shinto mythology as an alternative word for Kami. Amaterasu is called Amaterasu-O-Mikami and her brother is called Susano-no-Mikoto. There is no real difference in Shinto between Kami and *Mikoto*. So, as man is *Mikoto* he is likewise Kami. Man and divine spirit or Kami thus have the same meaning in Shinto. Man as *Mikoto* is self-creative and self-developing, not a mechanistic product of Heavenly Kami, but Kami or divine spirit itself come forth into objectivity. Thus Professor Katsuhiko Kakehi says:

> The word *Mikoto* signifies a being whether human or otherwise embodying Musubi. . . . Musubi is the essential source of creation, development and maintenance.[2]

The two original Kami of Growth in the Shinto mythology are called *Musubi*, personifying the creative impetus in its initial movements from subjectivity into objectivity. In seeking the basic Shinto meaning of the Japanese people as *Mikoto* or Kami, it is important to understand that *Musubi* is embodied in *Mikoto*, for it shows there is no aloof Heavenly power in Shinto of creation, development and maintenance controlling the people. The Japanese, in their inalienable Shinto personalities as *Mikoto* are individualistically self-creative divine spirit, or Kami, not dependent on omnipotence anywhere. Kami is not external to them but is them in objective form. W. G. Aston, too, defines *Musubi* in this sense, describing its Shinto meaning as "a power immanent in Nature and not external to it"; and he gives as examples the Japanese words *Musuko*, meaning boy, and *Musume* meaning girl.[3] Boy and girl, in the Japanese

---

[2] "Shinto," *Contemporary Japan Magazine*, March, 1933, pp. 589, 587.

[3] *Shinto: The Way of the Gods*, pp. 172-3.

language, embody *Musubi*. That is, they are in themselves, the essential source of creation, development and maintenance. They are *Mikoto* or Kami: Shinto divine spirit in earthly individualized form.

There can be no doubt, therefore, that in Shinto and in the meanings of archaic and modern Japanese words, the Japanese people are individualistically Kami or creative divine spirit on earth. To ignore this primaeval conception is to ignore Shinto. All the Japanese people are Kami. All the Japanese people, according to Shinto, are creative divine spirit: all are *Mikoto*. The Japanese people are the individualistic embodiments of creative divine spirit: *Mikoto* individualized.

What then, is the Japanese Sovereign? The same word, *Mikoto*, is used to describe him in Shinto as is used to designate the people of Japan, with an addition which identifies the Sovereign as transcending individualism. The additional word is *Sumera*, having the same root as the word *suberu* and meaning to unite as a whole.[4] The Shinto title of the Japanese Sovereign is

Every Japanese is *Mikoto*. The Emperor is *Sumera Mikoto*.[5]

Every Japanese, by Shinto, is creative divine spirit,, individualized. The Sovereign is creative divine spirit who unites as a whole. The Sovereign has his own individualistic personality; but in addition, as *Sumera Mikoto*, he is other than individual, he is the personalized unifying centre of the Japanese people and the Japanese nation. According to the modern *Gestalt* psychology, the whole is more than the sum of the parts. The whole ranks superior to all the individuals, for the co-ordinated oneness of the whole creates a new and higher condition than the unco-ordinated sum of all the parts. In conceiving the title of *Sumera Mikoto* for the Sovereign, Shinto shows the primaeval subconscious mentality possessed this knowledge of reality which only now modern psychology is coming to understand.

Sumera Mikoto was the title given to the first earthly Sovereign of Japan, Jimmu Tenno. Many centuries afterward, probably more than a thousand years later, the Japanese adopted Chinese ideographs and then they combined two Chinese characters to represent a Chinese expression for their Sovereign. The Japanese at that time were very much under Chinese cultural influences and often neglected the fundamental

---

[4] W. G. Aston's translation of *Nihongi*, p. 199.

[5] This is Professor Katsuhiko Kakehi's phrase, expressed to the author. See also his article "Shinto," in the *Kami Nagara Magazine* (Tokyo), July, 1932, p. 4.

primaeval expressions of their ancestors for foreign ideas, just as modern Japanese are charged with doing today. The ideograph they adopted for their Sovereign has the Chinese pronunciation of *Tenno*, and the Japanese, since then, have called their Emperors *Tenno*, which conveys the idea of Heavenly Self-Creative. The Japanese pronunciation of the Sovereign's title, however, still remains *Sumera Mikoto*, and this is the title used in the *norito*, the ancient Shinto forms of respect used in addressing the Heavenly Kami. The words *Sumera Mikoto* are the pure Shinto designation of the Sovereign, while *Tenno* is not.

Sumera Mikoto has a spiritual meaning as well as a nationalistic meaning of great antiquity which expresses the primal Shinto conception of the Sovereign far better than any imported words can do. *Sumera Mikoto* implies that the Sovereign unites as a whole the Japanese people as *Mikoto*, not only in their material characters as the inhabitants of the Japanese nation, but also in their spiritual relationship with Heaven. It is difficult to clarify this conception in the limited meaning of words. To understand the Shinto idea it is necessary to realize that in Shinto, Heavenly divine spirit expands from its subjective state into the objective universe in two forms—as individuals and also as a unified spiritual oneness. The subjective unification of divine spirit in the Heavenly source is represented in Shinto by Amaterasu. The objective extension of divine unification is personalized in Shinto by the *Sumera Mikoto*, the earthly descendant of Amaterasu. Shinto uses the simile of ancestorship to express this subtle primaeval conception, and no more simplifying form of words is available.

Western theology likewise employs the idea of Heavenly ancestry to explain mankind's relationship with Heaven. God is interpreted as the Heavenly Father in the West, but the idea is not extended to national spiritual unification: union between man and his Heavenly Father, according to Western theology, results only through forms of individual salvation or conversion prescribed by the priesthoods. The individualistic idea is predominant in the West. Western theology does not follow the concept of man's Heavenly ancestry in the self-creative, self-expanding way of Shinto. In the West, the Heavenly Father makes mankind apart from himself; but Shinto sees the Heavenly ancestral source self-generating into objectivity, never involving separation. Diverse individualistic forms emerge, but: at the same time there is also unified oneness. If the meaning is not clear to Western self-consciousness it is because respect for individualistic effort plays so dominating a part in

Western life that the subconscious intuition of inseparable spiritual entity is felt to be mystical and inexplicable. In Shinto, it is a natural and very real feeling. There are indications, however, that this primaeval intuition of monism and creative versatility is returning to Western self-consciousness through the influence of new scientific concepts. All the Japanese people, according to Shinto, have divine ancestry originating in spaceless Heaven. They are the diverse, individualistic centres of the evolution of the original self-creative source, which spreads outward through the continuity of earthly expansion of human life. The *Sumera Mikoto*, by the Shinto principle, represents an unbroken line of descent; from Amaterasu, the Shinto personality that means spiritual unification. Amaterasu, the Heavenly ancestress of the *Sumera Mikoto*, is more-than-materiality. When primal origins are sought, materiality vanishes, since matter has no original reality of its own. Behind the material universe, as its self-creative source, is pure immateriality. Shinto mythology gives a materialistic aspect to Heaven and to the Heavenly Kami, just as in the West, Heaven is described as having many mansions and pearly gates and being blessed with milk and honey, for the human mind is at a loss to know how to express the immaterial with material words. But, as modern science talks of electrons in words applicable to material things, although electrons have no materiality, so Shinto describes Heaven and Amaterasu and the other Heavenly Kami in a material sense, though the conception is really an other-than-material one. There is no representation of Amaterasu in any personalized form at any Shinto Shrine. Complete concealment, to suggest immateriality, is fundamental of the Kami representation at all Shinto Shrines.

Had Shinto simply established a tradition that in a material place called Heaven, material beings propagated the Japanese people, Shinto's spiritual influence could not survive. It is because Shinto's primaeval intuition realized that self-creative divine spirit comes forth into objectivity from the subjective source of the universe, called Heaven, that the spiritual value of Shinto has an all-enduring quality. The Japanese Sovereign becomes *Sumera Mikoto* when he succeeds to the title, No change takes place in his material ancestry as he mounts the Throne, but he becomes for the people of Japan the other-than-material descendant of Amaterasu, the divine unifying one of Japan. The *Sumera Mikoto*'s earthly ancestry unites him with the Shinto conception of Heavenly unified divinity, meaning that the all-inclusive oneness of divine spirit never has been broken from the beginning of time.

Here is no superstitious or mystical doctrine. The conception has high pragmatic value for Japan. The Japanese people feel their spiritual unification through the *Sumera Mikoto* as a realistic fact; and they respond to it with enduring advantage both to nationalistic cohesion and to their own spiritual contentment. The Japanese people subconsciously understand, without any necessity for self-conscious analysis, that through the *Sumera Mikoto*, they merge their individualities into a coordinated whole. How this influence works in Japan through the Shinto conception of the *Sumera Mikoto* cannot be self-consciously defined any more than science can explain how immaterial electrons become materialized. But it does work. The Japanese people know that for them, the *Sumera Mikoto* concentrates co-ordinated nationalistic and spiritual power throughout Japan, without which disruption would lend to run rife. The material handiwork of man is held together by material co-ordination of its parts. But, a subconscious living relationship has a unifying force that is subjective and not objective. When the Japanese successor to the Throne becomes *Sumera Mikoto*, a subconscious reaction takes place among the Japanese people which responds to the divine being who unites as a whole, without reference to his earthly body or to his individualistic private personality. He becomes the personalized centre of the co-ordinating impetus, cohesive in its effect, uniting the Japanese people in the spiritual sense of Shinto, which has a stronger unification effect than has any materialistic concept of a ruler's human power to hold his people together. The *Sumera Mikoto*'s unifying efficacy will continue as long as this element in the Shinto spiritual conception endures among the people who, themselves, conserve it. Though the Heavenly ancestorship of the *Sumera Mikoto* has inspired the Japanese people in the long past, modern self-conscious logic is at a loss to explain it:

> Those Japanese who in the twentieth century talk of the imperial visit to Ise as ancestor-worship art; sorely puzzled to justify their position. I mimed with the philosophy of China and the science of Europe they naturally find it difficult to understand how the Mikado can be really descended from the sun. Some resort to the Euhemeristic theory that she was a mortal Empress who lived in a place on earth called Takama no hara (plain-of-high-heaven) and speak of rice-culture and the art of weaving being known in her reign.[6]

---

[6] W. G. Aston, *Shinto* (in Religions Ancient and Modern Series), p. 27.

The philosophy of China has not saved Chinese spirituality from debasement, nor could the old science of Europe which Aston means, but which is now a discarded theory, explain Western spirituality. How, then, can they explain the Shinto meaning of the continuity of spiritual reality exemplified by respect for ancestors? When the *Sumera Mikoto* pays respect to Amaterasu at Ise, he expresses the spiritual oneness of Japan as indissolubly continuous with the spiritual oneness of Heavenly spirit. Those Japanese who are "sorely puzzled" by this procedure are modernized ones who have lost the subconscious intuitional Shinto knowledge of the past and have turned to the inefficiencies of modern self-consciousness in vain search of an adequate substitute. They are unfamiliar with the trend of the new science and philosophy of the West and are treading paths that the West is discovering lead into the jungles of both spiritual and material ignorance.

The *Sumera Mikoto*, as divine being who unites as a whole, pays respect not only to Amaterasu but also to all the individualized subjective personalizations of divine spirit as well. For, be represents both the spiritual impetus of unification in himself and all the individualistic appearances of divine spirit in Japan who become merged into oneness through him. This conception is very old in Shinto tradition. The Kogoshui, twelve hundred years ago, said:

> It is of prime importance for public morality that everyone should ceremoniously revere his own forefathers; therefore each August Sovereign when he ascends the Throne as a rightful successor of the Great Ancestral Goddess (Amaterasu), pays homage to all the gods (Kami) Heavenly and earthly.[7]

That is, each individual, as his personal act, reveres his ancestry which carries him back to his individualistic origin in Heavenly divine spirit. The *Sumera Mikoto* pays respect to all divine spirit as the unified whole of divinity, being himself the spiritual descendant of Heavenly oneness. So individualism and co-ordination are sustained and public morality benefits. Such meanings in Shinto must be subconsciously felt in order to be realized in any practical way. The Japanese, being so largely subconscious, have been able to cling to these conceptions by an inner knowledge not examined on the surface of the mind.

Yet, foreign ideas have crept into the Shinto principle of the *Sumera Mikoto*, at times, and have endeavoured to change its purely Japanese

---

[7] *Op. cit.,* p. 46.

basis as divine being who unites as a whole. Many people crave spiritual absolutism and search for a symbol to represent an omnipotent Heavenly deity to take care of their spiritual safety amid the material disruptions of life. Sujin drove any such implications from Shinto; but foreigners read their own interpretations into the Shinto concept of divinity and Kami, and they have exerted influences on some Japanese to follow them.

No idea of godhead can be associated with the Sumera Mikoto in the Shinto meaning. The first *Sumera Mikoto*, Jimmu, was a successful military leader and a co-ordinator. Had he been regarded as a god on earth when the Shinto tradition was being formed, it would have been impossible for the mythology to have related that he had to be rescued on one occasion by a "cross-sword" sent to him from Heaven, and that on another occasion he did not know where to lead his expedition and was guided by a Heavenly crow—that nearly led him into an ambush. Such are not the ways the primaeval mind imagines gods. Nowhere in the Shinto mythology is there any expression that can be interpreted as godhead in the accepted meaning of the word as divine power omnipotently applied; nor does the mythology provide any form of worship for the people. Amaterasu is not worshipped by the people; and whenever the mythology describes Heavenly conferences, Amaterasu does not control the situation like godhead but is attended by advisers who evolve the plans. The Shinto mythology shows clearly that the intuitional subconscious knowledge of the primaeval Japanese carried Shinto away from the self-conscious doctrine of godhead toward the far higher subconscious conception of the universality of creative divine spirit, which the modern mind is beginning to accept after experiencing the failure of the idea of a detached godhead to be permanently satisfying.

Shinto has established no godhead in Heaven for religious worship but regards the Heavenly Kami as divine ancestors. Therefore it is not Shinto to interpret the respect and veneration shown for the *Sumera Mikoto* as acts of religious worship. The *Sumera Mikoto* conception of Shinto is purely Japanese, having its origin in the subconscious knowledge of reality of the primaeval mind of the Japanese race. Shinto does not justify taking from the *Sumera Mikoto* the meaning of divine being who unites as a whole and substituting for it the idea of a religious deity on earth, separated and aloof from worshippers. Shinto would lose its primaeval significance if any such materialistic meaning were to be used to change the original spiritual conception. There have been innumerable self-consciously evolved ideas of godhead in Heaven and on earth imagined by humanity. There is only one *Sumera Mikoto* conception that has survived from primaeval times into the modern era—the Shinto intuition of self-creative divinity emerging from the Heavenly origin as individual *Mikoto*, united through the *Sumera Mikoto*. This unique character of the *Sumera Mikoto* is part of the Japanese Spirit. To reshape it so as to accord with foreign ideas of godhead would make Shinto an alien creed, like material things made in Japan after foreign patterns.

Sumera Mikoto is the most spiritually uniting title borne by any earthly ruler in its pure Shinto meaning that the people are spiritual in origin and become co-ordinated on earth among themselves through the *Sumera Mikoto* who also personifies for them the unified oneness of the nation with Heaven. The sustaining force in this Shinto conception is divine spirit as individually self-creative and yet always united. The idea of deity or godhead in Heaven or on earth, in any religious sense, means separation between the people and divinity in some form or other; but *Sumera Mikoto* means uniting as a whole.

Max Müller's opinion that "the belief in a Supreme Being is inevitable." is not borne out by the facts of Shinto.[8]

This is true, however, only in the sense of Supreme Being as aloof deity, which is the Western theological meaning. Shinto would be devitalized by any such doctrine which suppresses the Shinto intuition of divine spirit as universal, self-creative and self-developing, not mechanically controlled or made. But, Shinto embraces the principle of Supreme Being in the idea of co-ordinated divine spirit as more than the individual. The Shinto intuition sought to express this concept of Supreme Being personified as Amaterasu in a unified creative sense rising above the limitations of religious creeds. There is no conception of a Changeless Absolute in the primaeval idea of Amaterasu, whose Shinto position as Ruler of Heaven does not involve knowledge of the future nor control over humanity. Amaterasu represents the co-ordinated whole of divine spirit or Kami self-creatively expanding in its aspect of indivisible integration. The meaning of Supreme Being in Shinto thus does not imply omnipotence nor has it a theological purport. It is the verbal representation of co-ordinated creativeness.

According to the Shinto mythology, when Amaterasu hid herself in the Heavenly cave she did not know what was exciting the laughter of

---

[8] W. G. Aston, *Shinto: The Way of the Gods*, p. 69.

the Heavenly Kami who had organized a comic dance to persuade her to come out. The myth shows that Amaterasu possesses neither omniscience nor foreknowledge. She was excited by curiosity to emerge from the cave to see what was happening. Thus, in Shinto the conception of Supreme Being is shown not as a mechanistic principle but as a personality learning by experience—that is to say, who is self-developing. The Cave of Amaterasu is the Shinto burial tomb of omnipotence. When Amaterasu left the cave, a straw rope was stretched across the opening to prevent her re-entry. Its replica is used at Shinto Shrines throughout Japan. The straw rope forever bars omnipotence from Shinto, sustaining the primal Shinto conception of spiritual freedom and liberty for self-development of all individuals as superior to omnipotent mechanism.

Morality, virtue, general benevolence and all aspects of progress result as creative individualism becomes increasingly co-ordinated in advancing the united well-being of all. If there were no welding of diverse and disrupting individualism into co-ordinated oneness, humanity would still be in a primitive stage of existence. Individualism that holds aloof from coordination leads to evil and disaster. So, the *Sumera Mikoto*, uniting as a whole, thus may be said to personalize the fount of morality and progress which depend upon and grow with the development of co-ordination in human relations. When it is said in Japan that Shinto centres about the *Sumera Mikoto* this is what is subconsciously implied. Japanese, too, may speak of the *Sumera Mikoto* as "the one perfect being," in a similar sense. The intuitive meaning is that spiritual and material unification of the nation through the *Sumera Mikoto* gives to the people a direct conception of the integrated whole as the ideal of perfectibility which is not possible to acquire in terms of divergent individuals. Too, it emphasizes the Shinto principle that materiality is an aspect of spirituality, unifying material existence with divine spirit as an inseparable coalescence. At the same time, individualism remains a reality in Shinto, for individuals form a united whole as material embodiments of divine spirit moving forth in the objective universe. The Japanese people are individually *Mikoto*, according to Shinto, while realizing their unification through the *Sumera Mikoto*. Some people, however, do not understand the Shinto concept of Kami or divine spirit as coming forth from the Heavenly source through their individual personalities. They may concentrate the meaning of divinity entirely in the *Sumera Mikoto* and so shirk their own responsibilities as *Mikoto* for advancing the progress of divine spirit in their own environments. This idea is not Shinto but is due to the spread of foreign conceptions of divinity in Japan. Shinto exalts the *Sumera Mikoto* as the unifying whole above individualism; but Shinto also requires that every individual retain his own spiritual self-respect: as *Mikoto*, divine being on earth embodying musubi: self-creative power.

Some individuals, too, may interpret the Shinto conception of perfectibility in terms of their own self-assumed omnipotence. They may advance their personal opinions as being supremely wise and commit acts which they place beyond criticism on the plea that the *Sumera Mikoto* requires their aid to maintain perfection by any means they judge best. Shinto perfectibility, however, is personalized only in the *Sumera Mikoto* who unites as a whole, not in individuals cither surrounding him or at a distance. The *Sumera Mikoto* ideal of Shinto gives no omnipotent knowledge to anyone nor does it sanction any claim to absolutist sway over others. Otherwise, co-ordination would disappear in an anarchy of individualism, each individual trying to force his own opinions on his neighbours. Shinto means self-purification, not enforcement of purification on others.

The *Sumera Mikoto* unites the Japanese people spiritually and nationally. At the same time, in economic, social and political fields, the people struggle among themselves for co-ordinations of their own making amid the affairs of life, and so keep the creative impetus a vital power through individual effort. Shinto provides no earthly or Heavenly deity to direct these attainments.

> Plato believed that a nation cannot be strong unless it believes in God. A mere cosmic force, or first cause, or clan vital, that was not a person could hardly inspire hope, or devotion, or sacrifice; it could not offer comfort to the hearts of the distressed, nor courage to embattled souls. But a living God can do this, and can stir or frighten the self-seeking individualist into sonic moderation of his greed, some control of his passion.[9]

This belief, far older than Plato, is due to the cry of self-consciousness for consolation and to the self-conscious idea of separation between humanity and the divine. Deeper than the self-conscious surface, Shinto resides in the subconscious knowledge of reality where creativeness exerts its power. There is no cosmic force controlling the universe in Shinto. but divine spirit, itself, personalized in humanity, carries progress forward. Shinto inspires devotion and sacrifice through the *Sumera Mikoto*,

---

[9] Will Durant, *The Story of Philosophy, p. 35.*

for devotion and sacrifice are individualistic contributions to the ideal of co-ordination. No personalized deity is embodied in this principle, however. The Shinto conception is more profound and belies Plato by showing that a nation can be strong, hopeful, devoted and self-sacrificing without a Platonic God, for the people find in themselves individualistic divinity and in the *Sumera Mikoto* unified divinity on earth.

In other countries there is a legal principle that the monarch is above the law, expressed in the phrase, "The king can do no wrong." Here, too. is a subconscious ideal of perfection in the ruler; for as the personalized co-ordinated whole of the nation, the monarch is above individualistic offences—even though in his private capacity he may commit them—and so is above the law, which primarily is made to restrain individualistic excesses. In Shinto, however, the conception has a more emphatic significance because of the idea that the Japanese people are *Mikoto* while the Sovereign is *Sumera Mikoto*. The *Sumera Mikoto* can do no wrong since his perfectibility is centred in his spiritually unifying power which is felt subjectively in the hearts of the people. Wrongs originate when egoistic individualism and co-ordination fail to become adequately related amid the struggles of the people as individual centres of divine spirit. But, the *Sumera Mikoto* unites them in a spiritual-national synthesis despite the material struggles of life.

Shinto never has meant "divine right of kings" in the Western sense. This dogma is founded on a creed of omnipotent deity. If means that as Heavenly divinity is believed to control mankind and to be the maker of man and the universe by acts of omnipotent will, so the king, as the earthly representative of Heavenly omnipotence has unchallenged right to work his own will. Fundamentally, however, the doctrine of the divine right of kings springs from a primaeval subconscious intuition that sees a relationship between humanity and divine spirit, for the basic meaning is that the head of the nation is the national embodiment of: Heavenly divinity. To this extent, the principle is Shinto, but it loses the subconscious truth in the individualistic ambition of the monarch. In Shinto the primaeval truth has taken a different direction and one more consistent with the subconscious intuition for Shinto sees all the people as divine spirit individually and the *Sumera Mikoto* as the unifying spiritual centre of the nation: ruler and people forming an indivisible spiritual family. In the West, the doc-trine of "divine right of kings" has meant political absolutism culminating in the creed of the French Bourbons, *L'etat, c'est moi,* meaning the nation is the monarch's private property. Revolutions and reigns of terror have been the people's answers to such efforts to rob them of their own divinity and make divine omnipotence supreme in the ruler. In Japan, the *Sumera Mikoto* is the head of the nation, as the head of a spiritual family all members having common Heavenly descent. His will exacts unquestioned obedience but there can never be any Shinto principle of "divine right" in the Western sense of absolutist political domination over the people because the people and the *Sumera Mikoto* are one. The "divine right" of the *Sumera Mikoto* is not fundamentally dissimilar from the father's right as the head of his family, where all are one. So, in Japan, the *Sumera Mikoto* has seldom taken actual political power into his own hands after the formative stage of national evolution was ended. The example was set by the Sumera Mikoto Tenchi, who as Prince Nakanooe, had been one of the principal creators of the great Daika Reforms in the Seventh Century. He succeeded to the Throne in the year 661 but did not become *Sumera Mikoto* until seven years afterward.

> Having assumed the task of eradicating abuses which for a thousand years had grown unchecked, he shrank from associating the Crown directly with risks of failure. But in the year 668, judging that his reforms had been sufficiently assimilated to warrant confidence, he formally ascended the Throne.[10]

Here was no effort to assert the divine right of kings nor to display any idea of infallible godhead. To have taken the position of *Sumera Mikoto* before his individualistic work as a reformer seemed to have reached the co-ordinating stage would have made the Sovereign a partisan in politics. Partisanship disrupts the Shinto idea of *Sumera Mikoto* as the divine being who unites as a whole. If the people were to cease their political activities and accept political control by the *Sumera Mikoto*, as the normal way of government, the creative impetus of Shinto would become lost and omnipotent, absolutism would result. For, the people, as individualistic divine spirit play their essential parts in furthering progress, and through struggle and competition reach the right way eventually by experience and experiment. The *Sumera Mikoto* holds unification of the people steadfast during these struggles. As the co-ordinated centre of the nation, however, he is neither a public partisan nor a political propagandist. During previous centuries the Shogunate kept the *Sumera Mikoto* aloof from political complications, and constitutionalism acts in the same way now. The *Sumera Mikoto* is the nation's binding power, superior to

---

[10] Brinkley, *op. cit.*, p. 168.

changing political conditions. In his private capacity, the *Sumera Mikoto* holds individual points of view, like any other individual, as many Japanese Sovereigns who became Buddhists have demonstrated. But, as *Sumera Mikoto*, in their public positions, the Sovereigns always have followed the intuitive, subconscious way of Shinto by uniting the nation as a spiritual whole while the people have struggled among themselves to advance the cause of creative action.

The *Sumera Mikoto* and the Japanese people together thus jointly create in this sense the nation's progress. This fact was well understood by the Emperor Meiji, who held Japan so successfully co-ordinated during the unprecedentedly difficult period when the people emerged from mediaevalism into modernism. In his speech promulgating the National Constitution in 1889, the Emperor Meiji emphasized the part the people of Japan had played in laying the foundations of Japan and carrying the country forward (italics the author's):

> The Imperial Founder of Our House and Our Imperial Ancestors, *by the help and support of the forefathers of Our subjects*, laid the foundation of Our Empire upon a basis which is to last forever. That this brilliant achievement embellishes the annals of Our country is due to the glorious virtues of Our Sacred Imperial Ancestors *and to the loyalty and bravery of Our subjects, their love of their country and their public spirit*. Considering that Our subjects are the descendants of the loyal and good subjects of Our Imperial Ancestors, We doubt not but that Our subjects will be guided by Our views and will sympathize with all Our endeavours and that *harmoniously co-operating together*, they will share with Us Our hope of making manifest the glory of Our country both at home and abroad and of securing forever the stability of the work bequeathed to Us by Our Imperial Ancestors.

This address echoes the spirit of Shinto. It recognizes that the development of Japan has not been due to any exclusive Heavenly power in the *Sumera Mikoto* but to the Sovereigns and the people "harmoniously co-operating together." Such was the Emperor Meiji's interpretation of Shinto, which had played so vital a part in overthrowing the Shogunate system and giving Japan constitutional government. No claim to exclusive responsibility on the part of the *Sumera Mikoto* was made by Meiji. In one of his poems, Meiji wrote:

> Was it that the Kami made the Mirror to inspire man to develop his mind when looking into it? [11]

---

[11] This poem was set to music and was sung and danced in Tokyo, May 28, 1932, at a trial performance of new compositions for use at Shinto Shrine ceremonies.

The meaning is that mirrors have a Heavenly origin, designed to bring men face to face with their spiritual selves and so stimulate them to put forth effort for progress. The mirror, which is a spiritual symbol in Shinto, thus becomes a source of democratic inspiration for self-development for all the people. In the mirror they see themselves and in seeing themselves, see also the divine spirit, or Kami, which is their own personalities. The same basic idea may be discerned in the Emperor Sujin's action, two thousand years ago, when he caused the Mirror of Amaterasu to be removed from the Palace. Sujin apparently did not wish the Mirror to be regarded as giving him sole claim to Kami, divinity on earth. He showed a desire to bring about a realization of the universality of divine spirit and to stimulate the people to develop themselves by democratizing the Kami. In the poem of Meiji can be detected the influence of Sujin, continuing through the centuries in Japan, subconsciously keeping alive the Japanese people's capacities for self-effort and self-development.

The Emperor Sujin removed the false concept of omnipotent deity on earth from the *Sumera Mikoto*, emphasizing the necessity for creative action and self-trust. The way was thus cleared for the *Sumera Mikoto* to attain the Shinto meaning of spiritual co-ordination of the nation without interrupting the self-development of the people of Japan and not devitalizing individual initiative and co-operative effort. In the Emperor Meiji, this co-ordinating power of the *Sumera Mikoto* encountered modern conditions of life with impressive success, causing Japan to emerge from mediaevalism into modernism within a generation and with no disturbance of the national structure. The instinctive power of Shinto now unites the ancient spirit of the past with the new spirit of the present. through the *Sumera Mikoto*, As long as Japan holds to this Shinto principle of the *Sumera Mikoto*, the national creative spirit will be able to readjust itself to all changes that future progress will require, without undermining the ancient foundations that reach to the primal depths of universal divinity.

CHAPTER VIII

SHINTO INFLUENCES ON JAPANESE CULTURE

THE cultural evolution of Japan has been due partly to the importation of foreign ideas and customs; but they have always undergone modifications to a greater or less extent because of the persistent power of Shinto to hold the Japanese mentality to the path of creative progress and versatility of self-development. Had Shinto expanded into a self-conscious understanding of life with a comprehensive creative philosophy of its own, its effect on the general trend of Japanese culture would have been more definite and more easily discerned. Indeed, if Shinto had become self-expressive instead of continuing simply as an inner intuition, foreign conceptions of life would not have obtained such an important hold in Japan, for Shinto would have changed them more fundamentally than it has been able to do. Being essentially subconscious and intuitive, Shinto has had to exert its modifying creative power from within the Japanese mentality, not by processes of self-conscious analysis. This method has not been spectacular and has attained its results more by slow persistence than by provocative and challenging comparisons with the imported principles. To examine all the subtle influences of Shinto on Japanese culture would require detailed examination of every period of Japanese history. There are, however, many indications of the general trend of the Shinto remoulding power that show themselves near enough to the surface of the Japanese cultural currents to be readily discernable. Yet:

> At no time has Shinto produced a great propagandist. No Japanese Sovereign ever thought of exchanging the tumultuous life of the Throne for the quiet of a Shinto Shrine nor did Shinto ever become a vehicle for the transmission of useful knowledge.[1]

Shinto influences cannot be found through any search for formal propaganda. The depths of subconsciousness have been Shinto's working base. From the innermost recesses of the mind's knowledge of reality, Shinto has put forth its power, saving Japanese culture from becoming too much entangled in the death clutch of the unrealities and static formalism in

---

[1] Brinkley, *op. cit.,* p. 229.

imparted dogmas. And if Japanese Sovereigns preferred to retire to Buddhist Temples instead of to Shinto Shrines, it was because the desire for retirement was to seek self-conscious contemplation of life and death which Shinto never has encouraged.

Foreign conceptions of existence have been so largely influential in stimulating Japan's intellectual development because the Japanese themselves have never shown persistent competence to formulate the profound Shinto knowledge of reality in ways comprehensible to self-consciousness. The starved Japanese, intellectualistic mind has had to turn to foreign ideas, though fortunately for Japan's development, Shinto modified them at least in part.

The Japanese as a whole are not a people with much aptitude for deep metaphysical ways of thinking. . . . Abstruse conceptions of Chinese or Indian origin have been received into the Japanese mind just as they were preached, and usually we have not troubled ourselves to think them out again; but . . . have generalized them straight away and turned them immediately into so many working principles. . . . Ideals in their original home are ideals no longer in our island home. They are interpreted into so many realities with a direct bearing on our daily life. . . . We are, think, a people of the Present and the Tangible, of the Broad Daylight and the Plainly Visible. The undeniable proclivity of our minds (is) in favor of determination and action, as contrasted with deliberation and calm. . . . Pure reasoning as such has for us little value beyond the help it affords us in harboring our drifting thought to some nearest port, where we can follow any peaceful occupation rather than be fighting what we should call a useless light with troubled billow and unfathomable depth.[2]

The realistic meanings rather than the metaphysical subtleties in foreign ideas have carried them into Japan; and it is because Shinto itself is fundamentally realistic that the spread of speculative and mystical conceptions in the imparted principles has been checked. The Japanese look the ready-made doctrines of India and China, and revised them not by analytical processes but by instinctive reactions that emphasized some parts and subordinated others subconsciously seeking to fit them into the mental moulds that Shinto had stamped with its permanent impress. The fittings have never been perfect and often the foreign ideas have become misshapen; for the readjustments have never been self-consciously made. Blind feeling has been the method, for Shinto has groped its way through the Japanese mind, too often, with closed eyes. Nevertheless, both Buddhism and Confucianism became more practical and

---

[2] Kakuso Okakura, *The Japanese Spirit,* pp. 46-9.

more in keeping with creative progress in Japan than in their original homes. Buddhism died in India and Confucianism degenerated into formalism in China; but in Japan the creative influence of Shinto rescued them from such fates.

Shinto's subconscious emphasis on the reality of life, the self-development of the individual and the universality of divine spirit have had profound influence on the evolution of Japanese Buddhism. In Shinto, matter has no fundamental materialistic reality in the sense that matter does not originate in itself; but matter and material existence have reality as real aspects of divine spirit—indeed, they are divine spirit, not mental illusions. Objectivity is divine spirit, in Shinto, not an unreality. Objectivity is divine spirit become materialized by divine spirit's self-creative power of expansion. Original Indian Buddhism, however, regards individuality and the objective universe of matter as illusion. When this aspect of Buddhism is emphasized, pessimism and inaction tend to dominate the mind. For if man regards neither himself nor human causes nor material progress as real, effort declines. Shinto conceptions of realism are evident in the reason why Buddhism became accepted in Japan:

> The religion of Buddha was first adopted by the people (of Japan) to satisfy their yearnings for a beyond. . . . Teachings of communion and salvation . . . appealed to the people as a promise of eternal life to be enjoyed in community with kinsmen and fellow people in Buddha's paradise.[3]

Shinto never has satisfied such self-conscious yearnings of the mind, for Shinto never has been made into a spiritual philosophy of life; but it was the intuitive, inherited influence of Shinto's emphasis on realism that caused Buddhism to be interpreted as a way to gain real happiness after death, in terms of the reality of the individual. This is far from the original Buddhist principle which regards salvation as the result of complete elimination of individualism and absorption of the individual personality into the All Oneness of Nirvana. Annihilation of individuality, however, could not sustain itself in Japanese Buddhism, however much lip service was paid to the principle, because the creative spirit of Shinto had made the idea of the reality of individuality a permanent possession of the subconscious mind.

Early Buddhism in Japan tried to emphasize intellectualism, for the Japanese mentality had not evolved intellectualistic concepts of its own and was hungering for refreshment. But, the Shinto principle of existence

---

[3] Anesaki, *op. cit.,* pp. 7, 67.

is not intellectualistic. It arises from intuitional subconscious knowledge of reality, unanalysed and free of logic. So, there was constant subjective resistance in Japan to interpretations of spirituality based on intellectualistically conceived logical formulae. The Nara schools of Buddhism which turned toward intellectualism were checked by the Shinto intuition of practicality, despite the eagerness of the Japanese mentality for intellectual excitations. When Buddhist intellectualism was struggling to establish itself through the Nara schools of thought, the two authoritative books on Shinto mythology, the Kojiki and Nihongi, were compiled at Nara in the Eighth Century. Neither one shows intellectualistic analysis nor trained self-conscious coherence, but they contain intuitive knowledge of life inherited from primaeval times. Intellectualistic Buddhism had entered Japan one hundred and fifty years previously, but it had not succeeded in halting the power of Shinto to keep the Japanese mentality from falling a full victim to the corrupting influences of formal logic in spiritual matters.

Dengyo, the founder of Tendai Buddhism in Japan in the Ninth Century, at Mount Hiei, moved against the exclusiveness of the intellectualistic Nara schools by asserting that Buddha is both the objective and the subjective universe—the phenomenal world and also inner Reality. Intellectual Buddhism regarded the universe of matter as unreal and saw reality only in the pure subjectivity of non-existence. Dengyo's doctrine that Buddha is the objective world reveals the influence of Shinto subjectively emphasizing the reality of material existence as a spiritual fact. It may be said that Dengyo intuitively tried to combine inherited Shinto realism with Buddhistic principles. Realism was made very apparent at Mount Hiei by the turbulence of the Tendai monks who at times carried confusion into Kyoto by their militant descents—the inherited Shinto impetus of material action overwhelming Buddhist contemplation. Out of Tendai many sects have expanded carrying the Shinto principles of individual reality and universal spirituality into different phases of development. On Mount Hiei is a statue of Dengyo surrounded by the statues of eight originators of other Japanese Buddhist denominations having their roots in Tendai's subconscious Shinto influences, including Zen, Jodo and Shin, which with the independently developed Shingon, are the most progressive sects of modern Buddhism in Japan.

Kobo Daishi, the learned founder of Shingon Buddhism at Koyasan in the Ninth Century, tried to amalgamate Buddhism and Shinto. Though such movements always have failed to find a permanent all-inclusive basis for co-ordination, nevertheless Shinto has exerted much power in the formation of Shingon beliefs. Kobo Daishi asserted the material body of every individual is Buddha, awaiting development by disciplinary activities. The Shinto principle that man is Kami or divine spirit intuitively influenced this doctrine. Koyasan became a centre of mysticism and the secret tenets responded to the Shinto intuition of living reality, for according to the creed of Koyasan, Kobo Daishi never has died. He sleeps at the end of the Koyasan cemetery; and when the mountain priests attend him, they bow on leaving as to a living person. Indian Buddhism says the human body is illusion and life is unreal. Koyasan mysticism says the human body is living divine spirit—or, Buddha—and death is unreal, reversing the Hindu hallucination concept. Shinto emphasis on the divine reality of the living individual and Shinto abhorrence of death are thus mystically interpreted at Koyasan. The many torii in the Koyasan cemetery testify to the living Shinto influence on Shingon. Daisetz Teitaro Suzuki has pointed out that "Shingon knows how to appreciate the value of form" and he emphasizes too that "neglect of form is generally characteristic of mysticism."[4] Shingon's respect for form reveals subconscious Shinto promptings preventing Koyasan mysticism from overwhelming practicality: for interest in form always indicates responses to realism without which form would have only a negligible illusory interest for the consistent mind that regards the universe as unreal. In art forms, Japanese Buddhism pictures flesh and bone reality, not ethereal nothingness. Kobo Daishi largely contributed to this movement; and he showed still further the Shinto influence of practical realism by simplifying the Japanese syllabary.

The evolution of the idea of salvation in Japanese Buddhism has been much influenced by the subconscious Shinto conception that man and Kami or divine spirit are one. The progressive expansion of the doctrine of redemption covered more than six hundred years from the time of Buddhism's introduction in Japan in the middle of the Sixth Century to the time of Shinran Shonin in the Thirteenth Century. The Nara intellectualistic principle of Buddhism, exemplified in the Hosso school, denied the universality of salvation and declared there are individuals not possessing the Buddha-nature and who, therefore, never can be redeemed. Tendai Buddhism, which followed Kara Buddhism, extended salvation

---

[4] "Buddhism and Japanese Culture," *Eastern Buddhist Magazine*, June, 1933, pp. 119-20.

to all, but made it dependent on religious rites; and in the same era, Shingon Buddhism regarded even demons and all alien cultures as aspects of Buddha and so open to ultimate entrance into Nirvana through mystical rites. In India and China, some trades were denied to Buddhist laymen because of their supposedly detrimental effects on attainment of enlightenment; but after the Nara period of Buddhism passed, all trades in Japan were open to Buddhists, thus making everybody potential candidates for salvation.[5]

Following Tendai and Shingon Buddhism came the establishment of the Jodo sect in the Twelfth Century by Honen Shonin, who proclaimed salvation was automatically open to everybody, regardless of their merits or demerits, by simply calling Buddha's Name, reciting the phrase *Namu Amida Butsu*. Amida Buddha had made an Original Vow to save the universe, by this doctrine, and redemption came because of the Vow and by continuous repetition of the Sacred Name. In the Thirteenth Century, Shinran Shonin, founded the Shin sect and carried Honen's principle forward to its uttermost theological limits by proclaiming that no repetition of a religious formula is necessary for salvation which comes spontaneously by relying on Amida Buddha's Original Vow to save everybody,

> Shinran's religion may be called a kind of naturalism, in the sense that nothing is required on our part, whether effort or training or transformation, as the salvation provided for us by Buddha is simply to be accepted and relied upon without questioning or conditions. . . . Our destiny is entirely in Buddha's hands, is encompassed within his plan of saving all as expressed in his vows; nay, our salvation is predestined and well-nigh accomplished, because Buddha has already, millions of aeons ago, perfected his scheme of taking all to his Realm of Bliss. "Calling Buddha's Name" . . . is rather reminding ourselves of Buddha's "primaeval vows" already accomplished than thanking him in anticipation of the bliss to be attained.[6]

In formulating this creed of all-inclusive salvation, Shinran was under the subconscious influence of the Shinto principle that man and divine spirit or Kami are the same. Shinran used Buddhist terminology, for his mental development had been under Buddhist instruction; but he could not have emphasized Buddha's Original Vow in the way he did had he not inherited the subconscious Shinto realization of universal divinity.

---

[5] Information to the author from Professor Entai Tomomatsu.

[6] Anesaki, *op. cit.,* pp. 183-4.

Though the wicked continue wicked, they are saved nevertheless:

> Even a good man is reborn in the Pure Land (attains salvation), and
> how much more so with a wicked man![7]

This saying of Shinran means that a good man relies partly on his
good deeds for redemption, but a wicked man relies wholly on Arnida
Buddha's Original Vow to save everybody regardless of their merits or
demerits all of which are due to *Karma* and not to the individual; and the
Original Vow is the sole power for salvation. The essential factor in this
creed linking it to Shinto's subconscious influence is that the divine nature is not cancelled by evil deeds—though, as Shinran said, we ought
not to take poison though a remedy is at hand.[8] The emphasis on the
universality of salvation by no act of the individual makes the Shinran
doctrine the closest any Buddhist theology has come to the Shinto principle of universal divinity.

Shinran further showed the subconscious power of Shinto when he
enunciated his doctrine of once saved, always saved.[9] This saying was
not elaborated by Shinran and has been a stumbling block to many. It is,
however, Shinto realism put into ecclesiastical terminology. To be saved
in this sense means man never loses his spirituality, once he realizes his
divinity, regardless of his activities. Or, in the Buddhist phrasing, Buddha's Original Vow never can be retracted. It emphasizes the
Shinran-Shinto creed of universal spirituality. The inevitability of redemption for everyone can be expressed in Shinto terms by understanding
that universal redemption means the individual cannot lose his divine
spirituality. The Shinran conception implies the same thing, since if divine spirituality were lost by anyone, Buddha's Original Vow of salvation
for all would be nullified. So, Shinran was responding to the inner Shinto
inheritance of the Japanese mind when he said, once saved, always saved.
By Shinran's Shintoist interpretation of Buddha's Original Vow, man
may be sinful and so may retard the progressive development of spirit
on earth, but he cannot be other than divine spirit, whatever his activities.

Shinran was under Shinto influence, again, when he insisted on the
right of priests to marry and to eat whatever food they desire. Shinto

---

[7] *Tannisho,* translated by Tosui Imadate, p. 5.

[8] *Ibid,* p. 25.

[9] *Tannisho,* p. 31. The phrase is translated in the English edition of the *Tannisho* as
"once saved, never forsaken."

makes no difference in sanctity between priests and laymen; and at any Shinto Shrine a layman as well as a priest can administer purification. Shinto dislikes principles of spiritual differences between people, and Shinran was moving toward this same understanding of the universality of divine spirit in his efforts to humanize the priesthood. Zen Buddhism, too, shows Shinto intuitiveness of reality in many of its aspects, Zen emphasizes the divinity of the individual self and trusts to enlightenment as an inner process of the mind. Though Shinran regarded salvation as beyond the power of the individual to control, and though Zen sees enlightenment as coming from within, yet both tendencies of thought are congenial to Shinto in that neither conceives an aloof deity, arbitrarily granting or withholding redemption according to sonic Heavenly whim. Zen comes near to Shinto in its doctrine that attaining enlightenment does not mean retirement from the world of desires; for the enlightened Zen Master can mingle with whom he likes without loss of spirituality—a principle that makes some Zen Masters in Japan highly agreeable social companions through their versatility of interests and naturalness. Like the priests of Shinto, they are not in fear of contamination on occasions of relaxation.

Shinto has rescued Japan from being victimized by ecclesiastical doctrines of original sin and Hell. Buddhism has many Hells for punishment of the fallen, but Shinto has prevented them from having widespread terrorizing effect. Buddhist Hells in Japan have provided artists rather than theologians with material for professional use. Separation from the Unified All replaces original sin in Buddhism as the cause of evil. But, the Shinto insistence on the reality of the individual as a desirable and not detrimental spiritual fact of life has much mitigated in Japan the effect of this teaching. It has made the idea of salvation from original sin strange to the Shinto mind. Salvation, in Japan, has a meaning of universality; and this aspect together with the reality of the individual, has given to Mahayana Buddhism, as interpreted in Japan, its strong appeal to a culture which is so much under the intuitive power of Shinto. Shinto has provided for the Kwannon creed its congenial soil in Japan:

> Never will I seek nor receive private individual salvation; never will I enter into final peace alone; but forever and everywhere will I live and strive for the redemption of every creature throughout the world.[10]

---

[10] "The Pledge of Kwan-Yin," *Aryan Path Magazine* (Bombay), January, 1933, p. 21.

This concept is very old in Buddhism and did not originate in Japan. Nevertheless, the Japanese have accepted it at its full face value as a realistic doctrine, while elsewhere it has had a more philosophic than a popular influence. It is the intuitive Shinto sensitiveness of the universality of divine spirit that causes the Kwannon principle to be regarded in Japan as a natural statement; but when there is a theological creed of original sin to be overcome by direct human effort, the Kwannon conception is not acceptable. That there should be any lost souls in the universe is repugnant to the Japanese innermost feelings because of the Shinto influence. How to overcome the idea of spiritual destruction or backwardness in reaching a theologically defined spiritual state has greatly interested Japanese Buddhism not through philosophic reasoning nor by analytical ponderings but by direct understanding, for Shinto has always tended to turn the Japanese mentality in that direction. Honen and Shinran, seeing salvation for all through the direct desire of Amida Buddha, and Zen Buddhism regarding enlightenment as resulting through an inner realization, have both followed the Shinto intuition which turns away from the spiritual destruction of anyone. In Japanese Buddhism, enlightenment rather than salvation is the way to a state of spiritual contentment; and it is a term more in keeping with the Shinto conception. Enlightenment, however, need not be an intellectualistic process. Enlightenment can come through realizing that the mind itself, in its normal tendencies, carries one toward development of spirituality which does not have to be expressed in order to be understood, by an inner feeling.

Keizan, the founder of the great Sojiji Zen Monastery, at Tsurumi, near Tokyo, reached Zen enlightenment, as a young priest of twenty-two, when in the year 1290, he heard a sermon preached on the text: "The mind in everyday life is the path itself."[11] In China, where the phrase originated, the idea aroused intellectualistic interest. But, in Japan the principle has a direct meaning, not an intellectualistic one, for Shinto had prepared the Japanese mind to respond to such an idea, intuitively. The Shinto "path" or the ideal of life is the way the mind moves forward in every day life, struggling to overcome the daily obstacles of progress and seeking to advance not by dreaming vaguely of some possibility of the distant future, but by day-by-day accumulation of effort and

---

[11] See pamphlet in English, *The Sojiji,* issued by the Sojiji Monastery, p. 4. Professor Tetsujiro Inouye has informed the author that the phrase is attributed to Ma-tsu, of China (died 788 A.D.); but it may have originated with Chao Chou,. of China (died 897 A.D.). The literal translation is: "The ordinary mind, that is the way."

competence. It is the path of self-creative action. Here is an excellent example of what Kakuso Okakura meant in saying that "abstruse conceptions of Chinese or Indian origin have been received into the Japanese mind just as they were preached. . . . They are interpreted into so many realities with a direct bearing on our daily life." Shinto always has exerted this influence on the Japanese mind.

Zen displays the Shinto influence, too, in its doctrine that the deepest truths of life cannot be verbally explained and must be transmitted from mind to mind by an inner communion. This principle can be carried too far and can cause in some people mental indolence. But, it is the Shinto way of explaining the primaeval conceptions of life. Not by analysis nor by attempts at logical and philosophic reasoning but by innermost feeling and intuitive understanding has Shinto obtained its power in Japan. This is why the development of the Zen mentality has been more congenial and persistent in Japan than in other Oriental countries.

Zen's practical attitude toward life is likewise in keeping with Shinto. The creative spirit of Shinto ever presses for action and expansion of material attainments; and the discipline of mental powers of Zen has for its purpose the stimulation of efficient activity. When that factor is missing in Zen, as it sometimes is, Zen tends to lose its higher levels of attainment. The activist impetus in Zen showed special force during the Ashikaga period when Zen priests explored the trade markets of China, made reports about them to the Japanese governing officials and acted as commercial advisers, gaining profit for their own temples at the same time. The Tenryuji Zen Temple, at Kyoto, could not be constructed out of local revenues during the time of Ashikaga Takauji (1305-1358) but the Zen priests did not abandon the work. They were practically minded activists, not engaging in Zen processes of discipline simply for the sake of inner satisfactions.

> The Abbot Soseki devised a plan that a ship should be sent to China for foreign trade, and the profits thus gained should be applied toward the expenses of the temple construction. . . . And thereafter the Tenryuji sent out its merchantmen to China every year, and the expense of the construction was met with the revenues from the foreign trade.[12]

Tenryuji stands today, a perpetual reminder to Zen of the Shinto principle that the intuition of creative life points to utilitarian effort as a gain,

---

[12] Yosaburo Takekoshi, *Economic Aspects of the History of the Civilization of Japan*, Vol. I, p. 212.

not a loss, for divine spirit on earth. In the Ashikaga period, Zen Buddhism in Japan acquired an impetus of creative progress through material accomplishment by the Zen priests, themselves, that can be revived when modern Zen understands its partial affinity with Shinto.

The constant efforts in Japan to amalgamate Buddhism with Shinto, while never reaching a condition of true absorption, nevertheless gave to Buddhism the continuous proximity of the innate Shinto influence of creative action and self-reliance. It also permitted some expression of self-conscious spirituality to gain partial Shinto conceptions, from which Shinto likewise benefited. For Shinto widened its influence on the growing mental development of Japanese leaders of thought who acquired an original impetus for learning through Buddhism. This tendency never was adequately expanded, however as it might have been had Shinto been more self-conscious of its own inner values. The most serious inner struggle by Shinto against Indian Buddhism centred about the Buddhist doctrine of *Karma*—the past dominating the present and misdeeds in a previous state of existence having to be paid for by future reincarnations. Many Japanese have been detrimentally affected by the *Karma* theory in its fatalistic aspect. But, in general, Shinto's creative influences turned the Japanese mentality toward an inexpressive but potent conception that effects of the past can be overcome in the present by human effort creating a new *Karma* or by direct intervention of Buddha, The *Karma* concept, too, was kept in a practical channel by emphasizing the desirability of benevolence and righteous conduct. During any critical period in Japanese history, or when grave obstacles had to be faced, *Karma* was unable to check the spirit of creative action in Shinto taking command of the situation; but in quiet times, *Karma* tended to return.

Shinto had less difficulty undermining the debilitating influence of the Buddhist concept of life as unreality and illusion. In India, where the doctrine has been most persistently emphasized, escape from unreality has been sought by expanding the individual ego into the Universal All, considered as the only Reality. Not sacrificing the self, but magnifying the self to infinity has been the actuating desire. In Japan the influence has moved away from egoism toward self-sacrifice, especially emphasized in the code of the Samurai. The philosophy of life's unreality was interpreted among the Samurai to justify the offering of their lives for some cause in which they were interested—the cause itself being regarded as real. A sense of loyalty in terms of service that might lead to death was stimulated which gave to the Samurai an abiding reputation for unselfish devotion to their overlords. Thus, the same conception of the unreality of individual life led in India toward inactivity through the desire to overcome all earthly desires, while in Japan it led to an intensity of action by pointing to the fact that if life were an illusion it could the more readily be sacrificed for some worthy human purpose. The primaeval Shinto urge toward fruitful action must be accounted responsible for the difference.

The same Shinto power, holding the Japanese mind intent on activity, caused Confucianism in Japan to adjust itself to practical individualistic conduct instead of becoming simply a formal code of fixed rules of conduct. In China, Confucianism became sophisticated and was a subject for intellectualistic debate so that much of its most valuable principles of morality degenerated into lip service. Thus, the Confucian doctrine of loyally to the Throne never exerted in China the power that it did in Japan. The Chinese expressed their loyalty by bodily genuflections while they moved away from the co-ordinating influence of their rulers toward an extreme of individualism— from the effects of which China still is suffering. In Japan, the Confucian doctrine of loyalty was interpreted in terms of action and inspired many noble deeds of self-sacrifice. The Japanese, because of the Shinto influence, were never long contented with static interpretations of the Confucian principles.

The most determined efforts of the Tokugawa Shogunate to enforce the static Shushi school of Confucianism on the Japanese people, in order to support the *status quo* of the governing regime, ended in complete failure. The Shushi doctrine was interpreted as a restraint against new forms of activity, for it taught that action should be deferred until all possible future effects could be discerned. Indefinite postponement of progress is inevitable when it is believed no new move should be undertaken until every conceivable consequence is investigated in advance. In the Sixteenth Century, Wang Yang-ming, one of the few creatively minded Confucians that China has produced, attacked the Shushi school. He declared knowledge and action are the same, urging that new forms of action should not be delayed to await advance knowledge of results, for the knowledge would accompany the action. This creed showed the creative spirit at work in his mind. For a while the Wang Yang-ming doctrine was popular in China; but the Chinese mentality always has sought ways of evading the development of new effort necessary for new activities— otherwise China would not today be in the plight it is. The Chinese said Wang Yang-ming's interpretation of Confucianism was wrong because if knowledge and action were the same, it would not be necessary to acquire knowledge through study, since by action new knowledge automatically would appear. This conclusion being regarded as an absurdity, Wang Yang-mingism was rejected in China.

In the Seventeenth Century, the Wang Yang-ming interpretation of Confucianism passed into Japan under the name of Oyomei, through the efforts of Nakae Toju, a poor Samurai. The Shinto influence of creative action caused the Japanese to interpret the Oyomei idea at its fundamental value, not to philosophize about it. The Oyomei doctrine does not mean to imply that study should be neglected. It emphasizes that to study without acting is fatal. Furtherance of action should be the primary consideration; and as action basically depends on individual effort, the Oyomei school stimulated the desire for individual self-development and freedom which the Shushi doctrine was suppressing. The inner mind has knowledge of life, according to Oyomei, and can adjust itself to new conditions of activity. The basic influence of Oyomei, when rightly understood, furthers trust in oneself to act; and such self-trust engenders a sense of responsibility for the consequences of one's actions. It was the subconscious intuition of creative action and individual responsibility in Shinto that caused the Japanese thus to understand the fundamental conception of Oyomei. Nakae Toju indeed, seems to have felt this innermost association of the Shinto spirit with Oyomei.

> He even went so far as to advocate a compromise between Shinto and Confucianism. In "Shinto Taigi" he makes an interesting attempt to synchronize the two.[13]

But, however much Shinto influenced imported concepts of life in Japan, it never limited itself to any one of them; and Shinto remained independent. At the same time, the progress of the Oyomei principles in Japan coincided with a revival of interest in Shinto and the two movements became too powerful for the Tokugawa Shogunate to resist. Oyomei, in its own field, was sufficiently influenced by the Shinto spirit to give Confucianism in Japan a new impetus of action in terms of individual responsibility, and loyalty to the Throne, which caused it to play an important part in the restoration of the Emperor and the establishment of constitutionalism.

---

[13] See Galen M. Fisher's article, "The Life and Teaching of Nakae Toju," *Transactions of the Asiatic Society of Japan*, Vol. XXXVI.

Many indications of subconscious Shinto influence are present in Japanese aesthetics. Practicality and beauty are common associates in Japan, for the Shinto conception of creative action sees an increase of value when the aesthetic and the practical are united. The Ara-Mitama, the Rough Divine Spirit, and the Nigi-Mitama, the Gentle Divine Spirit, existing in the same personality, not dwelling apart, inspired Shinto from the beginning. The principle has contributed to saving the Japanese people from the debilitating consequences of over-indulgence in art for its own sake. Art and utilitarianism are more naturally co-ordinated in Japan than in any other country.

Rikyu, the great Tea Ceremony master of the Sixteenth Century, said that in laying out a garden, the proportion should be six of utility to four of beauty."[14] The Tea Ceremony, practised for many centuries in Japan as a performance of repose and admiration for aesthetic productions, has for its full purpose not only refinement of the artistic sense but also the disciplining of the mind and the development of powers of concentration for action. The small Tea Ceremony houses, isolated in their exquisitely delicate gardens, are set off by themselves to suggest temporary retirement from the confusions of life, as aesthetic enjoyment requires. At the same time security from eavesdroppers makes the houses admirable assembly places for secret conferences—which is not the case with paper-walled Japanese residences—and in former periods Tea Ceremonies served for this practical use. The Shinto spirit never desires to lose the sense of practicality in aesthetic environments.

Japanese sword-makers reached the highest levels of practical utility in their art, many centuries ago, attaining unsurpassed skill as swordsmiths. But, to be acceptable, the Japanese sword must be not only of the finest temper, it must also have elements of beauty. In addition, the Japanese mentality, under Shinto influence, gives a spiritual character to the sword difficult for foreigners to understand. The spiritual factor implies that the sword shall be used with a sense of responsibility and a desire for useful, not selfish, activity. The Japanese sword, in fact, represents the three creative characteristics of Shinto—spirituality, aestheticism and utilitarianism co-ordinated as one. No imported culture has ever modified this Shinto conception in Japan.

Japanese poetry shows Shinto influence in its form of expression. No elaboration, no expansive philosophy of life and no attempt to suggest

---

14 Matsunosuke Tatsui, *A Record of Famous Japanese Gardens,* reviewed by Eisaku Waseda, *Japan Times* (Tokyo), Oct. 30, 1927.

and solve riddles of existence trouble the poetic mentality of Japan. The Hokku, of seventeen syllables and the Tanka, of: thirty-one syllables have been the favourite Japanese ways of expression in poetry from ancient times; and the brevity of versification makes analytical efforts by the writers impossible. No similar forms of poetry exist in other cultures, just as no other culture has the spiritual concepts of Shinto. Subconscious intuition, not self-conscious reasoning powers, forms the basis of the poetry of Japan, as it does of Shinto. The Hokku and Tanka put forth subtle ideas, not fully developed, which the reader must interpret himself, as Shinto has been left for individual interpretations of its fundamental meanings. But, interpretation does not mean elaborate self-conscious understanding by the reader of a Japanese poem. The poetic ideas are well within the reader's mind and so are his intuitive additions. Feeling and attitudes and action, not analysis, are the responses that Japanese poems seek to develop; and it is the same with Shinto.

The brevity of Shinto, its lack of self-conscious coherence, has saved it from passing into control of theologians interested in making spirituality into formal creeds, to the exclusion of broadened views of life. Similarly, the compression of Japanese poetry into seventeen or thirty-one syllables has helped to save Japan from being led astray into exclusive interest in aesthetics. The Shinto power of practicality has broadened instead of deepened the stream of versification, whereby poetic interest has become widespread without dominating the Japanese mentality to the neglect of material things. As Shinto belongs to the people, themselves, so does Japanese poetry. Only the specialized mind can write the greatest Hokku and Tanka; but excellent versification is not difficult for the average mentality, and the short mode makes quick composition easy. Thus, the man of practical affairs can give some of his rime to poetic outpourings without neglecting his material activities. It can be said, therefore, that the Hokku and Tanka forms of poetry have facilitated coordination of the utilitarian and the aesthetic, the Ara-Mitama and the Nigi-Mitama in the Spirit of Japan. Elaboration and involved expressiveness have never found favour in Japan. The compression of ideas, initiated by Shinto, is carried to its extreme of innermost feeling in the nation's poetry—the oldest poems of the nation being found in Shinto mythology, which inspired them and initiated the condensed form Japan always has followed.

In Japanese literature, Shinto emphasis on vitality has exerted great influence. Death is often portrayed, but its hold on the Japanese imagination is due primarily to the activities that are so intense as to culminate in death. Indifference to death, not death itself, has been the theme. Action that disregards the threat of fatal ending or action that is pursued despite the inevitability of death exerts a fascination for the Japanese mind. The most popular dramatic episode in Japan is the story of the Forty-Seven Ronin who, in the Eighteenth Century, revenged the death of their daimyo by long, astute planning for a successful attack on the enemy in his Yedo (Tokyo) compound, against heavy odds. They disregarded the certain penalty of hara-kiri which they knew beforehand would be imposed on them for an armed assault in the Shogun's capital, and made no effort to escape after their victory. Their eventual deaths by hara-kiri emphasized the intensity of their resolute action overcoming all restraining obstacles; and for this the spirit of Shinto was responsible—the creative impetus of Shinto that pursues action and difficult accomplishments to the end.

The greatest literary work in Japan is Murasaki Shikibu's *Tale of Genii,* written in the Tenth-Eleventh Centuries, when Buddhist influences caused much interest in death and Buddhist magical rites at sick beds. Though Murasaki's genius for descriptive writing has not been exceeded by any novelist in the West, yet her art deserted her in a death chamber. Arthur Waley, the translator of *Genji,* points out that

> Murasaki has an inordinate fondness for death-scenes, coupled with a curious incapacity to portray grief. Her alertness suddenly leaves her. Usually she is interested in the different reactions of her characters towards a common situation, but in the presence of death, the people in *The Tale of Genji* all behave alike.[15]

Murasaki's fondness for death-scenes may be traced to the Buddhist teachings of her age which frequently show themselves in her writings. Buddhism and death accompany each other through her volumes. But, Murasaki's creative power was Japanese, and the inherited Shinto intuition of creativeness dominated her mind only in portraying living characters. She showed no self-conscious understanding of Shinto, but any work of genius is more subconscious than self-conscious in its source; and it was the expansive vitality of living persons that Murasaki sought to depict. As Shinto sees all action, whether good or bad, to represent the fullness of the spirit of life, so did Murasaki. Shinto does not think that the Ara-Mitama of divine spirit can become too rough while yet having

---

[15] *The Bridge of Dreams,* Vol. VI of Waley's translation of the *Genji* series, p. 14.

creative influence in life not to be neglected; and Murasaki was certainly in this mood when she defended herself in *Genji* for writing about characters who did not highly esteem virtue. All phases of life must be explored by life itself for the creative impetus to progress through experience and experiment. This Shinto principle is inherent in Murasaki's defence of realism in fiction:

> It used to be thought that the authors of successful romances were merely particularly untruthful people whose imaginations had been stimulated by constantly inventing plausible lies. But this is clearly unfair. . . . It happens because, the story-teller's own experience of men and things, whether for good or ill—not only what he has passed through himself, but even events which he has only witnessed or been told of—has moved him to an emotion so passionate that he can no longer keep it shut up in his heart. . . . There must never come a time, he feels, when men do not know about it. That is my view of how this art arose. Clearly then, it is no part of the story-teller's craft to describe only what is good or beautiful. Sometimes, of course virtue will be his theme and he may then make such play with it as he will. But he is just as likely to have been struck by numerous examples of vice and folly in the world around him; and about them he has exactly the same feelings as about the pre-eminently good deeds which he encounters: they are important and must all be garnered in. Thus, anything whatsoever may become the subject of a novel, provided only that it happens in this mundane life and not in some fairyland beyond our ken.[16]

The modern spirit of creative action and the Shinto spirit of creative action agree in this accurate analytical understanding of the art of great novelists. It is the inherited Shinto intuition in Murasaki's mind that causes so many critics to be astonished at the modern tone of her *Genji*—the intuition of life as creative effort. The "mundane life" of self-development creatively interested Murasaki, not "some fairyland beyond our ken." So, the necromancy of her time, the contemplation of the mystery of death in the unreal terms of Buddhist magic, could not spur Murasaki's creative powers of description, even though death chambers held her outward attention. The greatness of *Genji* is in its simulation of the unfolding of life as a moving reality, not overloaded with artificial crises written emotionally, but life moving forward naturally and never halted by individual crises nor by death itself. Murasaki seems to have felt her own incompetence to make death realistic, for she does

---

[16] *A Wreath of Cloud,* Vol. III of Waley's translation of the *Genji* series, pp. 254-7.

not describe the death of Genji, himself. He disappears from the *Tale of Genji* between the fourth and fifth volumes of the Waley translation, the latter opening with the terse announcement: "Genji was dead, and there was no one to take his place." Murasaki's interest in death was particularly of women, not men; and it is the activity of the feminine personality terminating in death that stimulates her creative genius, not the actuality of death, itself. In the feminine field this interest is not essentially different from the general Japanese interest in masculine activities that reach their highest dramatic form when they are so intense as to culminate in a tragic ending. It is not the tragedy of the death that fascinates, but the living purpose that has been served, either by some definite accomplishment or by inspiring others to put forth extremes of effort through loyalty to a cause, or by calling attention to acts of injustice or of baneful effect on public welfare. Such is the consequence of the Shinto intuition on the Japanese character.

Sei Shonagon, Murasaki's contemporary, also showed the intuitive Shinto influence of vital action in her *Pillow Book*. She was interested in the lighter side of life. Sprightly doings, quick repartee, virile feminine mentality, competence of a woman to hold her own in social relationships with men—such forms of realistic activities inspired her. That two such women as Murasaki Shikibu and Sei Shonagon should have risen to the highest literary eminence by describing life in mediaeval Japan is itself significant of Shinto's influence; for Shinto does not differentiate between men and women, as creative divine spirit, and encourages women to sustain their subconscious sense of self-respect and feminine self-development even though they be thrust into the background by inability of men to understand them. Buddhism taught that woman's salvation is impossible until she becomes reincarnated as man. But, in Japan, Shinto's intuitive resistance to such a demoralizing creed mitigated the debasing consequences of the doctrine far more than has happened in other Oriental countries where it has been preached. Had this not been the case, two such women as Murasaki Shikibu and Sei Shonagon could not have arisen in Japanese culture.

The Shinto conception of life as a self-developing, self-creative forward movement thus has ever served to save Japanese culture from succumbing to static or nihilistic influences imported from abroad or tending to rise within Japan itself. The instant understanding of Western scientific culture when Japan was reopened to the world in the middle of the Nineteenth Century is the most striking modern instance of this power of Shinto, which has endured intuitively for thousands of years in the Japanese mentality. The broad principle of self-creativeness in Shinto and the Shinto interest in novelty have made Japan a natural trial ground for changing interpretations of life from the beginnings of the introduction of foreign ideas to the present time. Shinto has welcomed any cultural explanation of life that interested self-consciousness except conceptions having mechanistic tendencies to move away from creative action. Shinto has opposed these principles, subconsciously, but without offering self-consciously evolved doctrines of its own. So, the culture of Japan still remains in the formative self-conscious stage of development, though intensively developed subconsciously. Shinto has yet to show its creative cultural powers in self-conscious terms. That is a major problem of the future which Shinto and Japan now jointly face.

CHAPTER IX

SOME SHINTO SHRINES

MAN piles stones on stones and believes he has made exclusive dwelling places for divinity whose spiritual inspiration increases with the wealth and adornment of the structures. Man forgets that divine spirit is universal and cannot be confined within walls nor by any power. But, Shinto does not forget. Shinto remembers that in the prehistoric past, the ancestors of the race gave the first impetus to humanity's realization of spirituality without the aid of edifices; and all that has followed since in Shinto rests on such primaeval directness. Nature invited primitive man to understand visually the universality of divine spirit that struggled for expression in the subconscious depths of the mind; and Shinto never has lost this first knowledge of Nature's spirituality.

Nature's spiritual communion with man preceded man's discernment that he, himself, is included within the spiritual whole of existence. Realization of the individuality of divine spirit on earth came forth from the subconscious mind after the conception of spiritual universality and is dependent on it. Whenever the spiritual comprehension of Nature fades, man severs spirituality from life and regards himself as dwelling apart from an aloof deity who must be appeased for man to become divine spirit—and then only after death.

Shinto, however, still comprehends the spiritual character of Nature and so makes no such artificial separation between man and divinity. Nature, not man, enlarges Shinto Shrines into sanctuaries of universal spirit. The lofty trees that surround the Shrines with abiding life lift their branches toward Heaven and induce a spiritual mood of all-inclusive divinity that denies mankind and Heavenly divine spirit are separated. There is no repression of divinity at Shinto Shrines. Divine spirit is not limited to the Shrines nor to man nor to Heaven. The Shrines are concentration centres for man's renewal of his understanding of the spirituality of all existence. Spirituality expands from the Shrines with the all-inclusiveness of Nature. Long before man offered his structural contribution to the Shrines, Nature made hers. Man's additions are auxiliary. The primal spiritual subconscious knowledge of Shinto needed no human craftsmanship to cause man to realize his divine identity with the universe. Nature pointed to this understanding and the intuitive power of the primaeval Shinto mind comprehended the meaning. The Shrine buildings came after, to emphasize man's right to his own place in the universality of spirit; but before man thought to give this accentuation to personalized divinity, Nature's Shrines were sufficient in Shinto to inspire him spiritually.

In Southern Kii, one of the centres of creative action in the primitive era of Japan, the Nachi Waterfall descends from a great height amid graceful, bowing foliage. The spray softly strokes the rocks and disappears into invisibility while the trees stand guard against pollution. The water follows its narrow downward way gently, with swift, smooth unconscious accuracy seeking its spreading goal beneath. The white threads of the falling current seem like ethereal coverings of purity, enveloping an inner spiritual power emerging from lofty Heaven into the universe beyond. Primitive Shinto regarded the falling Nachi stream in its cathedral setting of Nature's design, as an inspired spot, and called it Hiryu Shrine—the Shrine of the Flying Waterfall. No sacred building is there. Nature has given sanctity to the place; the universal spirit of Nature consecrated the Flying Waterfall for primitive man's spiritual refreshment. Today, still, the Shrine of the Flying Waterfall is part of Shinto with white-robed priests in attendance, for the Falls are Kami or divine spirit.

Why should it not be so? Has modern man so lost his understanding of the universality of divine spirit that the power of Nachi Falls to hold primitive man in devotional attitude of mind must be dismissed as a superstition of the past? Does modern man so neglect to pay proper respect to his ancestors who first saw spiritual values in life that he can regard the Flying Waterfall only as an aesthetic aspect of Nature? If so, modern man is spiritually the loser and moves away from the divine personality of the universe toward a debasing concept of materialism. He is loyal to universal divinity who bows before Nachi Falls, who holds himself spiritually inspired before its continuous yield of released, yet disciplined, energy, like some creative spiritual fount seeking earthly level for action.

Shinto regards the universe as Heavenly divine spirit coming forth into material form for the purpose of self-developing creative progress. Before man appeared on the planet, Heavenly divine spirit, according to Shinto, began its forward movement of objective action through the power of Nature. In this original impetus of the spirit of creative action, Heavenly divinity displayed its intent to evolve as the material universe for its own advancement in newly externalized fields of space. Nachi Falls, moving from quiet heights to its new level, far below, releases its energy for active effort. The ceaseless, sudden power, as it is viewed by Shinto, is spiritual in its source and form; and it inspires man to move from the still altitudes of inaction into the current of accomplishment, creating progress by self-effort as an obligation to the creative purpose of universal life. The Flying Waterfall priests of Shinto could say to man: here is Heavenly spirit's early effort at earthly activity; and the source of this divine energy is the same Heavenly source that is man's. The Flying Waterfall, itself, however does not think and does not speak. Man is the more progressive development of divine self-creative spirit, the more expansive attainment of the Shinto Kami. Yet, the further man advances in menial development, the more ought he to understand that the heights he climbs must not be allowed to separate him from the universality of divine spirit of which he is the fortunate earthly pinnacle. Without the base of universal spirit there would be no pinnacle.

If divine spirit never had attained self-competence in material form to develop as the waterfalls; if divine spirit had hesitated to plunge from placid security into the reaches of the uncreated and the unknown, the creative impetus of life never would have progressed to its human embodiment. But, because creative spirit undertook the great adventure of objectifying itself materialistically, and persisted in its course despite all the early cataclysms of inexperience, man has come into being, the heir of the universality of divine spirit in its objective formations. If creative divinity is universal, if there is no dualism in the universe, if all existence has an inner spiritual harmony, if truth was learned by prophets and poets who have touched the intuitive knowledge of life in many different environments and found the universe to be one, then primaeval Shinto was justified in paying respect to the spiritual inspiration of Nachi Falls. To regard the Flying Waterfall only as an aesthetic artifice of Nature is to limit one's own spiritual understanding.

Divine spirit, itself, is the Flying Waterfall. One can realize its presence there as one can realize the divine spirit of oneself if the vision be not lacking. But, to understand, it is necessary to comprehend the literalness of the Shinto conception that all the universe is divine and that every aspect is the self-evolved outcome of Heavenly spirit seeking objective self-development. To confine spirituality on earth to the human soul is to move in the dark of spiritual ignorance where the Flying Waterfall's divine nature becomes obliterated in the materialism of the self-conscious mind. The universality of divine spirit, if it be accepted, must follow the Shinto conception, and must admit Nature within the spiritual realm side by side with man, attributing Heavenly origin to both. If the universe is monistic, then the Flying Waterfall has divine origin, and man rightly pays it spiritual respect and feels his own soul broadening toward universality as he does so.

In the Yamato district of Japan, near Nara, is the Omiwa Shrine. A towering mountain is the divine spirit, the Shinto Kami, of the Shrine. In the far-off past, Shinto made the mountain serve as the Shrine and it remains as such today. One may say the Nachi Waterfall symbolizes Heavenly divine spirit coming down to earth; and the Mountain Shrine of Omiwa represents divine spirit on earth reaching upward toward the Heavenly source of life—the inseparable union of Heaven and earth in universal divinity. The great Gothic cathedrals of Europe are said by Oswald Spengler[1] to have been the outcome of Europe's conception of infinity in the Middle Ages. But, they more truly represent an effort by the clergy to hold infinity captive. Primaeval Shinto conceived infinity in terms of unconfined freedom; and represented the idea by paying spiritual respect to the living Mountain of Omiwa. It is not necessary for man to employ architects, builders and artists for the construction of a spired edifice in order to show his understanding of spirituality reaching into the measureless beyond. Such efforts often indicate not growth of spiritual conceptions but an expansion of utilitarian and artistic skill, and in addition a desire to control the popular mind by an organized priesthood seeking to magnify hierarchic authority. An evergreen mountain may represent the universality of divine spirit expanding into the infinite more effectively than a closed cathedral; and the mountain may hold the people to intuitive understanding of the universality of spirit more loyally than a formal creed. No cathedral erected by human hands can be made of the living spirit. When priests and people depart, the walls are silent and the stones and mortar are dead. Shinto, making a mountain into a primaeval cathedral, took the living spirit of Nature, and saw the cathedral not as an inert pile of matter but as creative divinity, itself come forth into objectivity from Heaven. Life is enduring on the slopes of Omiwa. From base to summit, the reality of life climbs ever upward, pointing toward infinity. The Shrine Mountain bears a full covering of trees, green with vital power the year round. They and their

---

[1] In his *Decline of the West*.

ancestors stood there before man appeared. Confinement of spirit does not hold in the Shinto Cathedral of Omiwa. The structure is one with expansive life: living spirit stretches forth its branches and sings of measureless divinity. So, Shinto impressed on primaeval man at Omiwa's Mountain Shrine the subconscious knowledge that the universe is a spiritual fact of living, expansive reality; and divinity on earth is more than man can contain within his own soul.

In the age of subconscious knowledge of divine spirit's universality, the divinity of the mountain was felt as a spontaneous intuition, not requiring self-conscious explanation. Now that self-consciousness has dimmed the primaeval understanding, modern man does not turn to the living mountain-side for spiritual inspiration but seeks to hold spirituality exclusively for himself to grasp. The mountain has become a victim of the self-conscious separation of life from divinity. Modern man is under the influence of the usurping creed of a dual universe. The mountain is seen as inanimate matter, and man regards it as debasing to associate a mountain with his own spiritual character, for he has been taught that spirit and materiality are eternally separated entities. But, not forever will such a doctrine carry man away from the spirituality of Nature. If, as Western science is saying, materiality has no fundamental reality and the universe seems like aspect of mind, then there must be a return in the future to an enlarged spiritual vision. When that time comes, the modern mind will understand self-consciously, the deep spiritual intuition of the universality of creative divinity that caused primaeval Shinto to turn to the living mountain to stimulate the living spirituality of man's own nature.

At Iishi Shrine, in Izumo, there is no inner Shrine building. Instead, a picket fence encloses a large rock. The rock is the Shrine of Iishi and people bow before it in spiritual respect. Its history has been lost in the primaeval past. Some say the rock represents the seat of the Kami divine spirit. Others say that in primitive times the rock was regarded as sacred. Whatever the original reason, the Rock of Iishi has been rescued from the oblivion where material logic has sent so many intuitive spiritual truths of the past. A guarded rock, holding a long tradition of spiritual inspiration, beginning when man first knew the universal divinity of existence, is as much entitled to respect as a quarry of marble turned into chiselled blocks to make an ecclesiastical structure. In Izumo, people pay respect to the primaeval rock, seeing in it a reminder of the all-inclusiveness of spirit, perpetuated from the remote ages of the human race. In the West, people have made a sacred hymn to the Rock of Ages and chant it for spiritual stimulation.

The Rock of Iishi is Shinto's Rock of Ages, holding the divine intuition of universal spirituality steadfast and inspiring man to understand not symbolically but in full reality, that the Rock is of divine origin, as much so as man. For, Shinto understands that Heavenly divine spirit objectified itself not only as human life but also as all materiality. Man gives thanks for the food he eats and attends harvest festivals acknowledging divine assistance in sustaining life. So man may properly pay respect to the divine spirit of the enduring rock that co-operates with the divine spirit of man by providing security for material activities. Divine spirit, according to Shinto, became itself the material of earth with which the creative spirit of man is bound in a co-operative union that permits humanity to endure in space. By such co-ordinations of its various aspects, Heavenly divinity has been able to objectify itself and engage in material self-development.

Science is beginning to find that there is an inner power of co-operation and co-ordination in Nature that points to an interrelated understanding of universal oneness. Primaeval Shinto implies the same thing by regarding the universe as the objective self-creativeness of Kami or divine spirit. Shinto carries the idea of symbiosis further than biology.

> In recent years biologists and others have emphasized a type of phenomenon known as symbiosis, which not only plays a profoundly important part in the evolution of organisms, individually and collectively, but . . . implies an interdependence, a biological reciprocity of organisms which appears to be essential to the continuance and well being of life. . . . There is, as Sir E. Ray Lankester has put it, a system of elaborate service of one organism to another. . . . The fertilization of plants by bees . . . and the nitrogenization of the soil by legumes, to the advantage of other plant life, are further examples taken at random from a long list which demonstrates that symbiosis, involving something very much akin to restraint and service on the part of the individual organism, is a cardinal factor in the evolution of living things.[2]

Symbiosis means much more in the Shinto conception of universality of creative divine spirit. The Rock of Iishi, representing creative divinity as the soil, properly receives man's spiritual homage for the part it plays in Shinto symbiosis by helping man. Could the rock do so, it might return

---

[2]   Hugh P. Vowles, "Modern Science and Purpose," *Hibbert Journal* (London), July, 1929, p. 650.

thanks with equal propriety to man, for man vitalizes the soil in exchange for the vitality the soil gives to humanity. Most of us become so individualized, self-consciously, that we forget our debt to the soil and regard a rock as only a piece of matter having no relationship with our sacred souls. To pay respect to a rock seems a sign of primitive ignorance from which our expansive selves have escaped into outer knowledge of things.

Shinto, however, still holds the inner knowledge; and Shinto continues grateful to the co-operation of the parts of universality of divine spirit that have given the part called man his opportunity to forge ahead in the universe. So, Shinto can be inspired by a solitary, ancient rock and does not have to construct cathedrals in order to make inert matter spiritually effective. The Rock of Iishi was man's first stone cathedral.

On the Rock of Iishi Shinto can stand to proclaim the universality of divine spirit. The Rock of Iishi is Heavenly divine spirit materialized in inflexible formation as man is Heavenly divine spirit flexibly intellectualized. Both are of spaceless spiritual origin and both co-operate in advancing the creative development of divine spirit in the spatial universe. Not to comprehend the profound meaning of this intuitive Shinto conception is to revert to dualism and plunge the mind into an abyss of material ignorance isolating man from the spiritual world in which he dwells. On the Rock of Iishi Shinto declares man is not an outlaw in the universe but is one with universal divinity.

Not at Nachi Falls nor at Omiwa Mountain nor at the Rock of Iishi does Shinto countenance theological worship of the Falls or Mountain or Rock. No spirit, no deity resides in them in any Shinto sense whatever. The Falls, the Mountain and the Rock are themselves Kami, self-creative divine spirit emerging from spacelessness and self-developing as the material universe; and man is the same in origin. This primaeval knowledge of reality marks the true greatness of Shinto in understanding the universality of divine spirit. It is pure monism. Shinto denies the dualistic doctrine that imagines a spirit in the Falls or in the Mountain or in the Rock. Kami, divine self-creative spirit, *is* Nature and also is all life, including mankind. There is no separation between the spaceless spiritual source of the universe and any of its objective aspects, any more than there is any separation between immaterial electrons and their emergence into material forms. Immaterial electrons and material elements are the same; and so spaceless divine spirit and Nachi Falls, Omiwa Mountain, the Rock of Iishi and man, himself, are the same. They are spaceless self-creative spirit externalized, and separated from one another in individual formation, but inseparable in spiritual origin. Man, bowing before Nature does not perform a religious rite, in Shinto, but pays respect to Heavenly spirit that is himself and more than himself, for it is the entire universe. If the Falls, the Mountain and the Rock were sentient, they, in turn, would bow before man, seeing in his difference from themselves enlargement of creative divine spirit beyond themselves.

Primaeval Shinto understood the fact of the universality of divine spirit in such ways, subconsciously, but never developed the truth self-consciously. Modern Shinto can learn the meaning self-consciously with the aid of the increasing trend of modern science which no longer sees Nachi Falls, Omiwa Mountain and the Rock of Iishi as things having fundamental reality of their own. Their reality is beginning to be scientifically discerned as aspects of self-creative mind or spirit—or, in Shinto phrasing, Kami. The more progress modern science makes along the spiritual pathway it is now discovering, the more will modern man begin to comprehend the enduring intuition of reality that caused primaeval Shinto to bow in acknowledgment of the divine co-ordination between humanity and the material manifestations of Nature.

As this understanding expands, self-consciously, modern Shinto, itself, will the better comprehend the universality of spiritual divinity that inheres in the respect shown to the Nature Shrines in Japan. They mark the beginning of Shinto's responses to the primaeval instinct of universal reality of divine spirit. Great initiating creative movements in human history are usually simple in their early formations and later grow in complexity. Each generation tends to respect its own additions or the inherited intricacies rather than the original source. Shinto has not moved in this way. Little development has occurred in Shinto since the primal intuition of self-conscious universal spirit came forth. Shrines of wood generally have been added to the Shrines of Nature's construction, but they do not replace Nature. The Shrine buildings always unite with the surroundings that Nature contributes. The buildings retain the simplicity of Nature and do not seek artificial adornments. They are primitive in design and construction, as though Shinto instinctively realizes that the primaeval intuition of universal spirituality must remain simple and direct to escape theological complications and misconceptions.

The Ise Shrine to Amaterasu, the most revered Shinto centre of divine unification, has the simple freshness, the gentle delicacy and the gleaming purity of a virtuous woman. Every twenty years the Shrine is constructed anew, as though to represent the ceaseless regeneration of the creative spirit and the feminine desire for perpetual youth—the continuous pressure of Shinto toward creative life and away from death. In the Shrine grounds, the Isuzu River flows as a living stream. It is stocked with fish, never to be caught; and when one dies in the water, haste is made to remove it as a pollution, for to Shinto death is defilement of life.

From woman comes forth life, and through woman humanity holds to the co-ordination of oneness in the family relationship, while yet expanding individually. Amaterasu, the mythological Ruler of Heaven, is a woman; and her enshrinement at Ise represents the Japanese people as a single spiritual family whose union takes its source in the co-ordinated divine spirit of Heaven, personalized in Heaven as Amaterasu and in Japan as the *Sumera Mikoto*.

Rightly did Shinto select womanhood in Heaven for this representation of the original source of unified divine spirit. Woman, as wife, is the centre about which the co-ordinated life of the family born in the present, is developed. But, this role never wholly satisfies the feminine nature. The wife never is exclusively loyal to her own home. She clings in loyalty to her parental home, as well, the home of the family born in the past. She seeks, likewise, a position in the homes of her children, who produce the family of the future. Without these three home loyalties, woman never is contented. As daughter, wife and mother, woman coordinates in her personality the past, present and future of the family relationship as a single continuity. So, Shinto follows the way of life itself in making Amaterasu personalize at Ise Shrine the unification of the Japanese people as a national family. Ise enshrines the life of the Japanese nation, past, present and future, united with the spiritual beginning in Heaven, as a continuous whole.

National accomplishments that bind the country together and prevent disruption are announced to the Shrine Spirit at Ise as one might announce to the mother a binding family success by the children; for Amaterasu personalizes the spiritual mother of Japan. After the Russo-Japanese War, when the Japanese people were saved from defeat at sea by Admiral Togo's naval triumph, the victorious commander made a journey to Ise with his staff and some of his sailors to pay homage to the Shrine where the co-ordinated, family unification of the nation is honoured. When Japanese officials are appointed to safeguard important national interests, they go to Ise and—if they rightly understand the meaning of the Shrine—they receive spiritual strength that subdues any desire for self-gratification and urges them to self-sacrifice if it should be necessary for the nation's benefit.

No omnipotent control over man is developed at Ise as a theory of existence. The Ise conception of life is based on the self-creativeness of divine spirit, emerging from Heaven into the spatial universe for progressive development. At Ise the fundamental Shinto conception is realized: "Kami Man not Two."[3] Ise is the people's Shrine in their collective capacity as the family of Heavenly divine spirit. It is, too, the Imperial Shrine, for the *Sumera Mikoto* is the earthly personalization for the Japanese people of the family head of the nation—the spiritual descendant of Amaterasu. The people of Japan as *Mikoto* and the Sovereign as *Sumera Mikoto,* are united in the indissoluble Shinto family relationship, whose intuitive spiritual meaning is refreshed by the Ise Shrine. To realize the meaning of this spiritual and practical unification which Shinto expresses at Ise is to understand that "Japan will endure as long as Ise endures."[4]

The Sacred Mirror which the Emperor Sujin removed from the Imperial Palace two thousand years ago, is kept at the Ise Shrine. It is the same Mirror which prompted the Emperor Meiji's poem urging the people to look upon it as an inspiration to develop their own minds. The Mirror of Ise thus is not a magical instrument for controlling the people. Its rays, reflecting the creative spirit of Heavenly divinity, do not point to any mechanically prepared way into the future, but reveal to man that he, himself, is creative divine spirit and must make his own way. Man has his divine ancestry, according to the Shinto understanding, not for the purpose of contemplating the Divine Mirror in reverent inactivity. Man is Heavenly divine spirit come forth into the objective world to engage in creative effort for individual self-development and to evolve co-operation in terms of human relationships.

The great Taisha Shrine, in Izumo, second in Shinto importance only to the Ise Shrine, represents this principle of Shinto. At Taisha, Okuninushi is enshrined. The masculine appearance of the Shrine, its hardy, vigorous character, distinguishes it from the delicacy and feminine refinement of the Ise Shrine to Amaterasu. The most conspicuous object at Taisha is a huge straw rope, entwined over the Shrine entrance. The straw ropes of

---

[3] This saying was written for the author by Rev. Ikashemaro Uda, Chief Executive and Assistant Chief Priest of the Great Shrine at Ise.

[4] Expressed by Ellery Sedgwick, Editor of *The Atlantic Monthly*, on visiting Ise Shrine.

Shinto Shrines bar omnipotence from the Shinto conception of divine spirit and represent by that fact human initiative and creative action. The straw rope of Taisha is much thicker than at other Shrines. It suggests extreme masculine effort, while its tightly bound strands indicate the power of co-operation. The massive, braided cable expresses the accomplishment of Okuninushi, the first human personality of great creative power in the Shinto mythology. He organized primal civilization in Western Japan, according to the mythology, and then agreed to unite his consolidated Izumo domain under centralized authority that included Kyushu and Yamato. The Taisha Shrine thus memorializes Okuninushi's local creative activities that culminated in Izumo becoming a part of prehistoric Japan, making Japan a co-ordinated state that has endured from Okuninushi's mythological era to the present time.

The Ise Shrine represents the spiritual unification of the Japanese race in the Shinto meaning of Heavenly divine ancestry. The Taisha Shrine represents the political and geographical unification of the Japanese race through the consolidation of Okuninushi's territory in the West with Central and Southern Japan—individual parts made permanently co-operative, through human effort. Amaterasu, the first of the Heavenly Kami, is enshrined at Ise. Okuninushi, the first great leader of earthly birth, is enshrined at Taisha. Each is Shinto Kami, divine creative spirit. To Shinto, divine spirit is always divine whether in Heaven or on earth, for man and divinity are the same. Neither Amaterasu nor Okuninushi, however, is an ecclesiastical god in Shinto. Each represents a different aspect of the Kami divine creative spirit. Amaterasu personalizes the oneness of individual Heavenly and earthly divinity; Okuninushi represents individual effort and co-operation of earthly divine spirit. They are not worshipped in Shinto, but respect is paid to them by living divine spirit whereby the subconscious Shinto intuition of spirituality in its different aspects rises nearer to the surface of the mind.

The Ise Shrine has the foremost position in Shinto because Shinto understands that the unified whole of divine spirit is primary and always endures, while the parts, in their objective, individualistic formations come and go. Yet, Shinto also knows that the divine oneness becomes diversified and individualized for the development of the material universe and the furtherance of divine spirit's objective progress through experience and experiment. All the Shinto Kami assemble at Taisha, every November, according to the mythological tradition, which still is recognized with solemn rites. The Kami hosts, meeting to pay their respects to the memory of Okuninushi, can be regarded as emphasizing the Shinto conception of the oneness of Heavenly divine spirit emerging into the universe through individualistic development and seeking earthly co-operation that yet will not destroy individualism. Individual Kami Houses at Taisha are reserved for the symbolic accommodation of the visiting Kami while they remain for a week at the Shrine of the human Kami commander of the past who consolidated the land. Individual personality is accentuated at Taisha. But, at Ise, the unified spiritual whole rises superior to all individuals.

Yet, even at Ise, near the Amaterasu Shrine, stands the Shrine to *Ara-Mitama,* the Rough Divine Spirit of creative action. Shinto never is forgetful of the fact that progress in life requires creative effort and disciplined resolve to overcome obstacles by the individuals who make the co-operative whole. So, Shinto never completes its enshrinements. New Shrines come into existence as posterity recognizes leaders who have guided the people in the quest for greater attainments. They are enshrined to perpetuate their influence and to emphasize that human effort is also divine effort having its originating impetus in Heaven.

The most recent of all Shinto Shrines is to the Emperor Meiji, in Tokyo, commemorating the leadership shown by Meiji when Japan created her modern civilization and left mediaevalism behind in the Nineteenth Century. The Ise Shrine sits far back in its surrounding park of great trees and shady paths, concealed until one suddenly comes upon it, as though it were in the world while yet also in the Heavenly realm of divine spirit. The Taisha Shrine nestles in a small town, half enclosed by a distant semicircle of hills, seemingly prepared for a projecting movement into the world of attainment lying beyond. The Meiji Shrine is in the centre of the great modern capital of Japan, approached along a broad, paved thoroughfare that leads from the crowded marts of the city where Japan's modern life is concentrated. The Spirit of Meiji looks on the new scientific development of Japan as accomplished fact. At Taisha, the Shrine of Okuninushi has the concentrated strength of primal man: primitive power, tense and straining to break forth, huge as the Shrine rope over the portal, reminiscent of a Rodin sculpture. At the Meiji Shrine, the impression is of human effort having gained disciplined control over its activities, self-assured and triumphant, self-contained and expanding with the accumulated ease of success.

Taisha Shrine and the Shrine of Meiji represent the continuity of the Shinto impetus of creative action, spreading forth from primitive beginnings into the modern world, carrying progress, through human effort, step by step across the ages. They mark the past and the present. At Ise, Amaterasu looks to the future, where increasing creative power depends on the primaeval spiritual intuition of Shinto continuing to endure in Japan and becoming self-consciously understood by the people.

CHAPTER X

SHINTO AND MODERNISM

SHINTO influences in Japan have been too long limited to the inner, subconscious mind. The modern age of intellectual development demands knowledge in terms of self-conscious comprehension as well as intuitive meanings. Shinto cannot remain simply a subconscious force if Japan is to increase her progressive development and retain her ancient culture. The suppressive characteristics of Japanese mentality must disappear under the pressure of modern education. Inarticulate idealism in Japan is ineffective for the modern world and is misunderstood not only abroad but also in domestic relations. The Japanese people must bring the intuitive knowledge of reality in Shinto to the surface of the mind for modern understanding. Otherwise, Shinto will go the way of other primaeval intuitive truths, as far as Japan is concerned; and over-individualism and blind materialism may then undermine the foundations of the nation.

Japanese culture has yet to pass into a developed phase of self-consciousness, self-expression and analytical originality. The Japanese people, hitherto, have sought in other cultures for self-conscious, self-expressive and analytical concepts of existence, ethical codes and scientific technique. The creative power within the Japanese race is very strong and has persisted for thousands of years; but it has not had the stimulus of a developed mental self-conscious sophistication. Japan has great capacity for originality, shown by Shinto and by the balanced relationship in Japanese culture of utilitarianism, spirituality and aestheticism. The fount of Japanese originality, however, irrigates chiefly the subconscious mind of the race. Originality in self-conscious analytical efficiency has always been rare in Japan. Adaptability to the self-conscious analytical discoveries of other races has been far more conspicuous throughout Japanese history than desire to analyse the fundamentals of Japan's own intuitive understanding of life.

The Japanese have vital contributions to make to world civilization when they learn how to explain the fundamental characteristics of their culture and train themselves in the advantages of analytical self-expression. As long as the nation remains mentally constrained and does not develop self-consciousness, the Japanese people will not play the part in the world to which their creative capacities entitle them. In the past, the Japanese intuition rightly turned from much discussion and moved toward action because the Oriental tendency was to rank discussion higher than action. The Japanese creative impetus reacted against this debilitating doctrine and saved the nation from being drawn into the Oriental vortex of inactive verbalism. When the choice is between words and action, words must be rejected. But, in the modern world, self-expression and self-conscious analysis have become indispensable aids to efficient action, for the complications of modern life and the new expansive relationships in human affairs are themselves due to increased self-conscious development of desires and extension of analytical capacities. To withdraw from self-consciousness and self-expression is to check progress, which is a denial of Shinto.

The Japanese people have accomplished extraordinary results through subconscious analysis and by intuitive responses to the Shinto conceptions of existence. Unsophisticated naturalness gives great charm to the Japanese personality. Gentleness, kindness and consideration for others are innate racial characteristics. Naive simplicity and open-mindedness combined with persistence in learning new things and disciplined intensity of purpose are common attributes of the Japanese mentality. But, some elements in modern Japan remain mediaeval still and social incongruities exist which are disconcerting at times. Insufficiency of self-consciousness, self-expression and self-analysis relaxes the mental processes amid the constant confusions of modern progress and checks quick concentration of thought on sudden problems. As long as self-expression and self-conscious analysis are underdeveloped in Japan, the mediaeval ideal of direct action, blindly conceived and confused in its methods and intents, will continue to dominate some of the people, working mischief to the nation at home and abroad.

The Eighth Century Manyo-shu has a poem by Okura Yamanouye: "Japan is the land where the spirit of language prospers." The implication is that the Japanese language has an inner spirit of comprehensiveness which the Japanese people intuitively understand. This is largely true; but the complexities of modern life demand more from language. Japan must become the land where the spirit of language is self-consciously analytical and stimulates self-expression and encourages quick mental originality. The primaeval desire for creative self-development is apparent in the Shinto mythology. Shinto requires self-expression, not suppression, of its fundamental tenets in order to be understood. Shinto has been laconic in its own explanations of its inner meanings because the Japanese mentality has not developed self-analysis; but the pressure of Shinto is toward open-mindedness and broad tolerance and indulgence. It encourages new experiences and experimental tests in advancing the cause of progress and self-development. Under modern conditions of life, self-expression, self-consciousness and self-analysis are essential for these desires of Shinto to become realized. Some Shinto scholars in Japan have vaguely realized this truth and have tried to develop self-expression but their influence has not become generally effective. Motoori Norinaga, in his *Kojikiden* comments on Shinto, gave a temporary impetus to self-expression. His great disciple, Hirata Atsutane followed him, being bold and striking in stating his convictions, and some others were influenced by Hirata's example. But another school derived from Motoori, led by Ban Nobutomo, inclined toward academic study and lacked vigorous self-expression.[1] The latter attitude, which has been general in Japanese culture, cannot carry Shinto into the modern era and sustain it there. The Japanese have a saying: "If you don't speak you will be morally suffocated." Shinto will be morally suffocated if the Japanese do not acquire more self-expression and self-conscious analysis.

The Japanese people can become self-consciously aware of the spirit of their own culture only by comprehending Shinto in modern ways of self-expression. There is a growing belief in Japan that the nation has gone too far in adapting itself to Western ways. This cannot mean that modern progress has reached desirable limits in Japan for the Japanese people still have much to do before their living conditions become satisfying to themselves. There can never be too much progress in Shinto as long as materialism is balanced by aestheticism and spirituality. The meaning is that the Spirit of Japan must not collapse before the enticements of Western materialism. This is true; but the Spirit of Japan cannot be saved by neglecting progress. It can be vivified in modern life by self-conscious understanding that the Spirit of Japan and Shinto are allied. Both have ever sought expansive ways of life, not static, mechanical conditions of existence. The young men and women of modern Japan are yearning for self-consciousness and are reaching toward analytical self-expression; but competent instructors for them are few. Teachers of youth in Japan, are, themselves, new to self-consciousness and are not

---

[1] Information to the author from Dr. Ryusaku Tsunoda.

trained in analysing the development of creative power in Japanese history nor in self-conscious understanding of the creative forces in the Spirit of Japan and Shinto. Chinese philosophy, Indian mysticism and Western science are better comprehended, in detail, among Japanese scholars than is the creative spirit of Japan, for Chinese, Hindus and the Western nations have self-consciously analysed their own processes of life, which are open to the world for examination. The Japanese people have shown creative competence in reshaping the self-conscious ideas of other cultures and in reorganizing modern Japan, industrially, financially and politically after Western models; but their overdisciplined self-restraint, their cloistered self-consciousness, have checked their understanding of their own subconscious creative originality. The effect is seen socially as well as in the practical activities of life. The Japanese deprecate themselves too much and artificially control their emotions. They are naturally expansive and are continuously alert, mentally, ever seeking ways of new activity. But, they hamper themselves by the false idea that confinement of the ego is the social ideal. So they have remained subconscious and subjective in understanding the creative expansiveness of Shinto, and do not self-consciously realize that Shinto has more adequate principles of spirituality, better fitted for modern life than Hinduism; is far more profound in its innermost philosophic concepts than Confucianism, and reconciles material progress with spiritual idealism in more stimulating measure man the West has been able to do.

It is time for Japanese scholarship to interest itself in the creative impetus of Japan's own culture. Modern Japan never will understand, self-consciously, the Spirit of Japan and Shinto by continuing to remain under the domination of Chinese intellectualism, Hindu philosophy and Western materialism. The advantageous elements in these foreign cultures should not be abandoned; but Japan must seek fundamental inspiration for her future progressive development by original creative analysis of her cultural evolution and by self-conscious comprehension of its vital power. The secret of Western success for which Japan has been searching since the Meiji era is in Japan, not outside. It is the same creative force that is buried in the Spirit of Japan and Shinto, except that in the West, it has been made self-conscious, objectively analytical and self-expressive, Japan, however, does not yet understand this truth because the people have restrained themselves too much and have given too high rank to silence. They have looked to foreign countries for self-conscious satisfactions of the mind; and their search for some secret way of life that they think gives the West its impetus for progress is due to their own lack of self-conscious understanding of themselves. The West has one immense superiority over Japan. The West is self-conscious of itself, analytical of its own past and ever seeks to develop higher competence in self-expression so that it can bring new ideas to the surface of the mind for objective examination and exchanges of opinion that result in widened knowledge. Japan has superiority over the West in intuitive feeling and subconscious understanding of life; and in Shinto Japan has a conception of universal creative spirit more realistic than the spirituality of the West. But, under modern conditions, self-consciousness, self-expression and analytical efficiency are more competent to develop human welfare than is inner feeling. If Japan is able to retain her intuitive and subconscious powers and at the same time develop self-consciousness, self-expression and analytical competence, Japanese culture will be carried to heights not yet reached by any other nation. But, the Spirit of Japan and the creative conceptions of Shinto will lie in a sub-conscious morass, increasingly ineffective to aid Japan's future progress, if the Japanese mentality continues to look beyond Japan for self-conscious inspirations, instead of developing originality of self-consciousness within the nation itself.

Revaluing the Spirit of Japan and Shinto does not mean reverting to reactionary ways of life. Some Japanese seem to imply that modern progress is detrimental to the Spirit of Japan, and they appear to desire the nation to return to the restraining simplicities of the past. Such people fear higher standards of living will cause Japan to lose the inherited sense of discipline and loyalty and the nation will become disinte-grated. The Spirit of Japan is not so weak that it cannot hold itself together as the people better their positions in life. The creative impetus of Shinto does not rest contented in perpetual poverty when ways of overcoming economic distress are ca-pable of being developed. Shinto sees divine spirit advancing as the people advance. But. in Japan, as in every other country, there have always been critics apprehensive of national degen-eration when the people aspire to higher conditions of welfare for themselves. Such pessimists place a halo of idealism on the past. Present-day Japanese speak of the Samurai Spirit of the past as the ideal. The Samurai Spirit has been of great value to Japan and is rightly considered one of the glories of the nation. Yet, this is what Muro Kyuso, a famous critic, born two hundred and seventy-five years ago, said of the Samurai Spirit of his own time:

Until the middle part of the middle age, customs were comparatively pure though not really righteous. Corruption has come only during this period of government by the Samurai. A maid servant in China was made ill with dismay when she saw her mistress, soroban in hand, arguing prices and values. So it was once with the Samurai. They knew nothing of trade, were ceremonial and content. . . . Even in the days of my youth, young folks never mentioned the price of anything; and their faces reddened if the talk was of women. Their joy was in talk of battles and of plans for war. And they studied how parents and lords should be obeyed and the duty of Samurai. But nowadays the young men talk of love and gain, of dancing girls and harlots and gross pleasures. It is a complete change from the customs of fifty or sixty years ago. To be proud of buying high-priced articles cheap is the good fortune of merchants, but should be unknown to Samurai.[2]

The Samurai of Muro Kyuso's time, learning the value of money, were pioneers preparing their class for Japan's expansion in the Nineteenth Century when the Samurai were abolished and had to turn to trade in order to live. Muro Kyuso was alive when the Forty-seven Ronin performed their memorable feat of Samurai loyalty; and their success was partly due to the ability of Oishi, their leader, to secure possession of their lord's fortune and judiciously expend it in the cause of retribution. Indeed, Muro Kyuso, himself, named the Forty-seven Ronin *Gi-Shi*, "Righteous Samurai," by which title they have since been known.

The progressive attainments of the present must not be misinterpreted in Japan by those who want so laudably to gain an understanding of the past. Development of self-consciousness, self-expression and originality of analytical research in the present are necessary if modern Japan is to understand the Spirit of Japan and Shinto in their influences on the nation. Japanese in the past no more self-consciously understood Shinto than does the present generation. Dazai Jun, a Japanese Confucian scholar of the Eighteenth Century, declared:

In recent times there has arisen a school of rationalists who say that the gentleman, being enlightened by reason, has no delusions about gods (Kami) and spirits. They would throw over the gods and spirits altogether; some of them alleging that gods and spirits are a theory invented by the sages as a device for governing the people. These rationalists do not know the way of the gods.[3]

---

[2] Quoted by Rev. G. W. Knox, *A Japanese Philosopher, Transactions* of the Asiatic Society of Japan, Vol. XX.

[3] Quoted by J.C. Hall, "A Japanese Philosopher on Shinto," *Transactions* of the Third International Congress on the History of Religions, Oxford, 1908.

Similar criticisms against modern Japanese youth are made today by people who imply such an attitude of mind never existed before in Japan. They say indifference to Shinto is due to modern material progress distracting the people's attention from the Spirit of Japan. They do not realize the true reason is lack of self-expression and deficient analytical ability. To turn from progress is not to return to the Spirit of Japan but to move far from it. As new methods of increasing production for the benefit of the people become known, Japan would be stultifying her own creative powers and the Spirit of Shinto if she were to neglect them. The Japanese have a proverb: *Hin sureba den sura,* "Poverty makes a man stupid (thievish)." To abolish poverty is to increase wisdom and honesty. The Emperor Keidai, who ruled Japan between the years 507-531 A.D., issued a decree saying:

> We have heard that if men are of fit age and do not cultivate, the Empire may suffer famine; if women are of fit age and do not spin, the Empire may suffer cold. Therefore is it that the Sovereigns cultivate with their own hands, so as to give encouragement to agriculture, while their consorts rear silkworms, themselves, so as to encourage the mulberry season. How, then, shall there be prosperity if all from the functionaries down to the ten thousand families neglect agriculture and spinning! Let the officials publish this to all the Empire so that our sentiments may be made known.[4]

The creative impetus of Shinto, seeking prosperity for all, spoke in this proclamation; and to good purpose, for in the reign of Keidai's successor, the Emperor Ankan, "the most noteworthy feature of his era was the establishment of State granaries in great numbers, a proof that the Imperial power found large extension throughout the provinces."[5] So, a return to the Spirit of Japan and to Shinto does not mean antagonism to Japan's materialistic expansion. It means understanding material progress in spiritual terms that will hold the people more closely together and will stimulate their sense of loyalty.

To become self-consciously aware of the creative spirit in Shinto will widen freedom and will check disrupting activities. Shinto is pure democracy. There can be no more fundamental conception of democracy than the Shinto principle that man and Kami or divine spirit are the same. The Shinto conception of universal spirituality confers spiritual equality on all. This does not mean, however, that everyone is equally entitled to

---

[4] *Nihongi,* translated by W. G. Aston, Vol. II, p. 5.

[5] Brinkley, *op. cit.,* p. 120.

lead the people or to teach them or to engage in public activities. The democracy of Shinto is creative democracy. It means that progress comes through self-development; and those who have self-developed themselves most adequately and have stimulated their talents most effectively are the ones who should lead the people toward new fields of expansion and national greatness. Shinto does not justify license being given for importing into the nation foreign ideas antagonistic to the national spirit and planting them in the untrained minds of young men and women. The Japanese mentality has an inherited facility for interesting itself in any fresh foreign theory as a self-conscious novelty. This fascination for external concepts is due to the fact that the Japanese have not developed their own Shinto philosophy nor analysed the Spirit of Japan self-consciously: so, original principles usually enter the Japanese mentality from abroad. To rebut alien conceptions not in accord with Japan's own cultural development, the Japanese usually rely on inner feeling and intuitive sensitiveness to the national spirit. But, uttering the word *Yamatodamashi,* "The Spirit of Japan," as an all-sufficient answer has not proven everywhere satisfying. Modern education causes Japanese youth to desire self-conscious analytical knowledge of their inherited culture in order to reject alien enticements by objective reasoning. Seldom is the material ready for them, for the Japanese people know themselves and their traditional ways subconsciously but not with sufficient analytical understanding for self-expressive use. So, when foreign principles that disturb the mind are circulated in Japan, many young Japanese become interested not because they comprehend the teachings but because they are not taught ways of refutation in self-conscious sophisticated terms based on the Spirit of Japan and Shinto.

The subconscious, intuitive processes of Japanese mentality cause new ideas to lodge in the innermost recesses of the mind where the thoughts they engender are concealed until they try to emerge with sudden explosive force. Self-expression and self-conscious analysis keep ideas in the open, for disciplined examination and gradual readjustments so that their errors and harmfulness are plainly discerned. In free Western nations, self-consciousness has been highly evolved for centuries, and the people have an inherited ability for self-expression and self-analysis. They are not shaken by freedom of entry being given to foreign ideas that conflict with their own racial conceptions. In addition to the national subconscious spirit there is a national self-conscious spirit which knows how to value foreign ideas by disciplined, objective analytical thought. In such nations, the people can be left safely to judge new social principles.

They have won the right *by* acquiring self-conscious capacity for analysis and self-expression, and experience shows they justify the indulgence of the governing authorities charged with protecting national welfare.

The tendency of disturbing ideas from abroad to hide secretly in the minds of Japanese young intellectuals produces a situation having dangerous elements. Professors who give tacit endorsement in Japan to foreign ideas that might cause national unrest are revealing their inability to understand the philosophy of Japan's own culture. If they understood, there would be less need in Japan for government supervision of "dangerous thought." The problem of "dangerous thought" in Japan is not basically a problem of scholastic liberty. It is fundamentally a problem due to the past inadequacy of Japanese scholarship to develop a self-conscious, analytical philosophy of the Spirit of Japan and Shinto. Subconsciously, the inner meanings are comprehended; but, self-consciously this is far from true. "Dangerous thought" is the outcome of self-conscious deficiency in understanding the Shinto Spirit of Japanese culture. Until Japanese scholars show they are competent to give self-expression to the creative spirit that has made Japan the great nation she is today, they should be cautious about instructing the young generation in new and untried ideas which the scholars take from alien cultures having standards of life differing from the Japanese. The way for freedom of thought to be established in Japan is to develop self-consciousness, self-expression and self-analysis. No new thought will be dangerous to the Spirit of Japan when the Shinto culture of the nation is made self-conscious to the people.

Shinto has intuitive knowledge of reality and is imbued with the creative spirit of life. But, the Japanese people have not yet understood their inheritance in this way by direct analysis. Shinto's intuitive power has kept Japan progressive, but the people do not know this is so, self-consciously and they are perplexed and confused in the modern world when they try to understand themselves by outward examination. Always they are told to look within; but modern life wants outward comprehension of itself to prove the inner, subconscious impetus is right. Japanese who discard Shinto as archaic because they do not understand it, are lagging behind the procession of modern progress. They do not realize it, however, because Shinto has not been made self-expressive. They have difficulty in believing their remote ancestors understood reality. They should understand that

   . . . our gratitude is due to the nameless and forgotten toilers, whose patient thought and active exertions have largely made us what we are. . . . Of the benefactors whom we are bound thankfully to commemorate, many, perhaps most were savages. . . . We are like heirs to a fortune which has been handed down for so many ages that the memory of those who built it up is lost, and its possessors for the time being, regard it as having been an original and unalterable possession of their race from the beginning of the world.[6]

The fortune of intuitive knowledge of reality, in Shinto, will be dissipated unless Japan becomes self-consciously aware of its value. Many other fortunes of the primaeval subconscious racial mind, like fortunes of inherited gold, have been exhausted by other cultures through lack of appreciation of their worth. Civilization tries to advance too often by the magnetic power of new ideas that draws the people away from memory of the past and causes them to struggle blindly for new adjustments which despoil the inherited instincts of true cultural progress. The tendency among modern young men and women of Japan to be indifferent to the past, however, means only that they do not understand their inheritance. They do not want to disown the Spirit of Japan; they feel subconscious pride in it. But, they are seeking to become self-conscious, and they can turn nowhere for explanations of Japan's cultural power in self-expressive, modern analytical terms. They begin to wonder, therefore, whether Japan's past has been creative or whether it is based on primitive ignorance that drew their ancestors away from realism toward mythological and mystical ideas of no value for the modern mind. Finding so little self-conscious analytical explanations of Japan's past adjusted to modern self-expression, they turn for realism to foreign cultures where self-conscious explorations of life are more interesting than the subconscious feelings on which they must rely for explanations in reading the Shinto myths.

> In comparing many of the youth of the present day in Japan with those of fifty years ago . . . about the ages of seventeen or eighteen many of them seem to begin to lose all sense of the beautiful ancestral and bushido teachings handed down to them so carefully and do not at all realize how precious they are. . . . Nay, they seem to regard them as silly! . . . These things being so ... I do not wonder at all that the Uji Cult (respect for ancestors) is being modernized and revived as a counter to this dire state of things. Some foreign missionaries and native pastors regret this, I know; but I am unable to do so. ... We find the first step in the Uji Cult to be common ancestor or clan worship. A worship

---

6 Sir James George Frazer, *The Golden Bough,* One Volume Edition, pp. 263-4.

said to be merely by way of respect and honor. The kannushi—Shinto priests—insist on this and call it *keirei,* "salutation." ...In this way ... is ... the whole race welded into one grand union with the gods (Kami). And to my mind this cult has been throughout the ages an unspeakably valuable and powerful national asset, . . . I believe it to be this fundamental and deeply grounded habit of mind in the Japanese people which has made them so strong, loyal and patriotic; and they have always been subconsciously so. The Japanese well know that so long as such principles hold the heart and mind of the people there can be no danger from outside harmful new thought. . . . But what they wish for is not the old expressed cult but the same cult on a modernized plan and in well explained terms clearly defined.[7]

Dr. Batchelor, engaged in Christian missionary work in Japan for more than fifty years, and highly trained in self-conscious analysis and self-expression, sees clearly the fundamental meaning of the ancestral cult in Japanese culture and its great value to the people. But, the modern youth in Japan cannot do so because it has not been explained to them; for most of their teachers have not developed self-conscious analytical competence to explain the creative aspects of the Spirit of Japan and Shinto. The young men and women of Japan, coming into modern life, have a right to ask for the meanings of their inherited culture in modern terms. They never will be contented with instructions to accept the doctrines of the past devoid of modern explanations. They should not be contented to do so, for their demands for explanations are an important contributing factor in urging the development of self-consciousness, self-expression and original analytical ability in Japan. Shinto cannot be forced into the hearts of the people nor can the Spirit of Japan be made a compulsory principle, unexplained and left isolated from self-consciousness in the subconscious mind.

If the Japanese people do not learn the meanings of Shinto self-consciously, the West will take their great spiritual inheritance from them. The Japanese did *not* appreciate their *ukiyoye* pictures until Western art specialists, through self-conscious analysis, saw the superb beauty and the spirit of the reality of life in them. Now, Japanese pay large prices to recover their own treasures, ignorantly sold in the past to foreigners. A similar humiliation for Japan will happen with Shinto unless the Japanese people self-consciously awaken to its value. Already the West is beginning to discern the spiritual importance of Shinto. In 1923, the

---

[7] Archdeacon John Batchelor, D.D., "The Ancestor Cult of Japan," *Pan-Pacific* (Tokyo), March 6, 1930.

Missionary Education Movement of the United States and Canada issued as a textbook for American and Canadian Sunday Schools, *Creative Forces in Japan,* by Galen M. Fisher, who had long been engaged in social work among the Japanese. The book says:

> Shinto reflects the genius of the Japanese people. . . . Not an iota of its beauty, its mysticism, its reverence for nature and for past generations should be lost. They all can be conserved and treasured by the Christian. And who shall deny that the Christian Church in Japan and elsewhere would be the gainer by incorporating the true and beautiful aspects of Shinto, shorn of superstition and narrow nationalism? [8]

This is the way Christian Sunday Schools in the West are beginning to study Shinto. Wider understanding and definite influence will come when Shinto's conceptions of divine self-development, universal spirituality and its general agreement with the new tendencies of modern science become more generally known. Mr. Fisher criticizes Shinto because it

> does not plumb the depths of the human heart or answer its longings and struggles. Like the exquisite shrines standing in groves apart, the Shinto faith seems to dwell apart from the bustle and strife of real life. [9]

Shinto does not stand apart from real life, for it has given to the Japanese race its intuitive responses to existence in ways of creative action, self-development and comprehension of the universality of divine spirit. But, it is true that Shinto has not answered the appeals of the heart for comfort and help amid the struggles of life. Shinto seems to be isolated in its groves because it has never reached the self-conscious surface of the Japanese mind and never has been interpreted to respond to the questionings of self-consciousness. Its "narrow nationalism" is due to the fact that Shinto began as an explanation of the history of the Japanese race's origin and early development, and expresses its intuitive knowledge of reality in terms of the Japanese nation. This, however, is fundamentally no more than a method of presentation. Everything that is basic in Shinto can be explained in ways applicable to the universe, not only to Japan. "Narrow nationalism" is not Shinto because Shinto is universal in its concepts. Those who interpret Shinto as being limited to Japan in its comprehension of life do not understand Shinto. There still are superstitions associated with Shinto Shrines—as, for instance, distribution of charms—but they are due to foreign influences, especially

---

[8] Galen M. Fisher, *Creative Forces in Japan,* pp. 109-12.

[9] Galen M. Fisher, *Creative Forces in Japan,* pp. 111-12.

Chinese, and they have been associated, too, with Buddhism in Japan and with Christianity in the West. The superstitious element in all progressive cultures is certain to disappear with increasing education.

Internationalism is being influenced in Japan through Shinto. At Yokohama, work was begun in 1932 on a private Shrine, erected by Kenzo Adachi, ex-Minister of Home Affairs, in memory of Christ, Buddha, Confucius, Socrates, Kobo Daishi, Nichiren, Shinran Shonin and Shotoku Taishi. The last four Japanese leaders, brought into this modern association with Christianity, Confucianism and the Socratic wisdom of Ancient Athens, indicate how the Shinto understanding of the universality of divine spirit is enlightening the Japanese mind.

Here is a beginning, but it must spread among the people; and it must be expanded into self-conscious comprehension of the full meaning of the Shinto knowledge of reality. Shinto has given to the Japanese people the impetus of creative action from the beginning of the formation of the nation. Yet, at Shinto Shrines action has not been developed. Inaction in general, prevails there. The Shrines, for the most part, have not become centres for helping the people to understand what Shinto means. They are places where the people go to pay respect to divine spirit and give "salutation" to universal divinity. The people have to find for themselves at the Shrines the meanings of spirituality. The Shinto priests pay formal respect to the Shrine Kami by food offerings and organizing festivals; but this is not enough to keep Shinto vital and cause it to be understood in all the deep fundamentals of its intuitive spiritual knowledge.

The Shinto priesthood has some men of splendid character, broad-minded, deeply interested in progress and desirous of expanding the influence of Shinto among the people. But, there are also Shinto priests of little education, small understanding of the meaning of Shinto, and incompetent to be instructors to the people or spiritual guides. Their salaries are insufficient to support them and their families and they are forced to do other work, in many cases, to give their dependents the common comforts of life. Shinto priests should be more than keepers of the Shrines, and they should have greater responsibilities for stimulating an understanding of the Shinto conceptions of life. Sacred dances, sacred music (which is partly Chinese), periodical food offerings, occasional festivals—these are not enough under modern conditions of life to give Shinto an adequate and permanent influence on the self-conscious minds of the people.

Education now is widespread in Japan. The people everywhere are literate. They rightly are wanting to know more of the meaning of Shinto in educated ways. They want to retain their educational self-respect and they will not be forever contented with the lack of progressive ideas at the Shinto Shrines. The Shrines must become self-expressive. They must help the people and not remain incoherent, when the people ask what Shinto means to themselves and to the culture of Japan. Such a development, however, can come only if the Shinto priesthood realizes its responsibilities in the modern era of increasing enlightenment. If the Shinto priesthood does not develop leaders among its number who can stimulate a modern interest in Shinto, then the laymen, themselves, will have to undertake this work or Shinto will lose its power over the Japanese race. Higher education for Shinto priests, in general, is essential for the welfare of Shinto. A wider cultural influence must expand from the Shrines; and the people of Japan must look up to Shinto priests as men competent to clarify the universal spirituality of Shinto in ways that will meet the requirements of the modern mind and provide an impetus for national and individual self-development.

There are some enlightened Shinto priests who understand this necessity. Already, a movement is beginning among them to introduce into Japanese schools instruction in Shinto along modern lines that will give to the young students some knowledge of their great inheritance. But, it is not enough for Shinto to be taught adequately in the schools. Adult minds need instruction, too; and the proper place for it is the Shrines. The creative aspect of Shinto, its universality of spiritual conceptions, its broad-minded tolerance, its influence on Japanese culture and on racial co-ordination all require self-conscious elaboration, not as a religious doctrine but as the national spiritual culture of the Japanese people.

The Spiritual Culture Research Institute, opened in Tokyo in 1932, marks a beginning in the field of exploration that has promise for the future. Japan never has evolved a self-conscious contribution to world thought of prime importance. The Spiritual Culture Research Institute has in Shinto the basic material for such an offering in exchange for what Japan has taken from the self-conscious cultures of other races. If Shinto be adequately explained to the world, Japan will have made a return balancing all that she has received from the world in the past, and more. For, once the full meaning of Shinto be realized by the world, it will vitally influence all progressive conceptions of spirituality, in every enlightened culture, and will rescue divinity from the burial mounds of intellectualism and materialism.

THE END

Printed in the United States
By Bookmasters